Collectors' Guide

Vintage Souvenir Tablecloths and Linens

Pamela Glasell

Photography by Glenn L. Glasell and Pearl Yeadon

4880 Lower Valley Road, Atglen, PA 19310 USA
Printed in China

Dedication

For my grandparents, Robert and Doris Erny, who taught me the value of hard work and a good laugh and make me proud to be an "Erny."

For my husband, Glenn, for his love and encouragement. And of course, for my children, Matthew and Michelle, whose love is my greatest treasure.

Acknowledgments

I have many people to thank for assisting me in the preparation of this book. Special thanks to the members of the "Vintage Tablecloth Lover's Club" for their friendship and support.

Thanks also to my mother, Pearl Yeadon Erny, for showing her true photographic talents in the fabulous scenic tablecloth pictures for the book and creating all the whimsical vintage linen crafts.

Copyright © 2004 by Pamela Glasell
Library of Congress Control Number: 2003112761

Designed by Mark David Bowyer
Type set in Zapf Humanist Dm BT/Souvenir Lt BT

ISBN: 0-7643-1978-7
Printed in China
1 2 3 4

Published by Schiffer Publishing Ltd.
4880 Lower Valley Road
Atglen, PA 19310
Phone: (610) 593-1777; Fax: (610) 593-2002
E-mail: Info@schifferbooks.com

For the largest selection of fine reference books on this and related subjects, please visit our web site at
www.schifferbooks.com
We are always looking for people to write books on new and related subjects. If you have an idea for a book please contact us at the above address.

This book may be purchased from the publisher.
Include $3.95 for shipping.
Please try your bookstore first.
You may write for a free catalog.

In Europe, Schiffer books are distributed by
Bushwood Books
6 Marksbury Ave.
Kew Gardens
Surrey TW9 4JF England
Phone: 44 (0) 20 8392-8585; Fax: 44 (0) 20 8392-9876
E-mail: info@bushwoodbooks.co.uk
Free postage in the U.K., Europe; air mail at cost.

Contents

Introduction

All I know is that with the approach of summer there comes an increasing yearning to set eyes upon far-off places at the end of the open road. This call when answered is usually termed, "a much needed vacation."
—Elon Jessup, *The Motor Camping Book,* 1921.

I have wonderful memories of my family's annual vacations. We would drive twenty-seven hours straight from southern California to the rustic family cabin on Flathead lake, Montana, only pulling off the road on adventurous, unplanned "gypsy trips" when an interesting billboard beckoned us from the road. We'd visit the "House of Mystery" or a "live alligator farm," investigating the new attraction, stretching our legs, and, of course, buying a souvenir. I still love to travel and I still love a good quirky souvenir. My cupboard is filled with interesting items from my travels: salt and pepper shakers, towels, aprons, and of course, linens.

I have only recently discovered the joys of collecting vintage souvenir linens. The first treasure was an old 1930s California souvenir tablecloth, found at a garage sale. Wrinkled and dirty, it took careful cleaning to reveal a wonderful piece of nostalgia, recalling the glory days of Hollywood and beautiful, pristine sandy beaches.

Currently, prices and demand for these classic treasures of our past have risen sharply. More and more collectors are drawn to these wonderful cloths, bringing the glorious past to their contemporary kitchen tables. I hope you will enjoy seeing them gathered together for this book.

The values in the price guide section were taken from a variety of sources, including on-line auction sites, vintage souvenir linen collectors, and antique dealers. The values assigned to the tablecloths shown are in a range from "good condition" to "mint with the tag." If the tablecloth you have is significantly damaged, subtract 25% from the lowest value given for a more accurate value. Enjoy!

—Pamela Glasell

Chapter 1

History of the American Tourism Industry

What could be more symbolic of America's past than the open road? An unbroken expanse of land with a solitary road disappearing into a vast landscape calls forth images of romantic waywardness and infinite grandeur. From nineteenth-century "pilgrimages" to Niagara Falls to 1950s cowboy dude ranches, tourism has been vitally important to the development of American culture and commerce. Tourism has transformed and reshaped not only the American landscape, but also our concept of America and how we defined ourselves as "Americans."

No sooner had the Wild West been "won," than tourists followed the covered wagons and railroads into the newly opened wilderness to experience the adventure and to settle and create new opportunities for themselves and their families. Between 1830 and 1850, many new American attractions, including Niagara Falls, the White Mountains, and the Adirondacks, became well established as fashionable tourist areas. The creation and marketing of these attractions, the development of adequate modes of transportation by trains and steamboats, and the growth of a leisure ethic are what made American tourism so popular in the late 1800s. As these areas grew and prospered, entrepreneurs realized that they were also attractions that could also lure sightseers, provide extra income, and encourage a constant influx of new citizens. In order to take advantage of America's new tourist economy, many communities in the United States reinvented or enhanced their own history, and roadside tourist attractions were born.

American Magazine, 1954.

This is most evident in the once sleepy ghost town of Las Vegas, Nevada. Vegas was the first town to legalize gambling in 1931. During the Great Depression, this insulated the young town from the economic hardships that wracked most Americans in the 1930s. Jobs and money were prevalent because of Union Pacific Railroad development, legal gambling, and construction of the Hoover Dam some thirty-four miles away in Black Canyon on the Colorado River. The success of the first hotel, "The El Rancho," triggered a small building boom in the late 1940s, including construction of several hotels and casinos fronting a two-lane high-

1950s Las Vegas "Vegas Vic" tablecloth. $95-$125. *From the collection of Jorene Uluski.*

way leading into Las Vegas from Los Angeles. That stretch of road evolved into today's most popular tourist destination in Nevada: the Las Vegas Strip.

Few inventions have had as great and widespread an impact on the development of America as the automobile and the national highway system. At the beginning of the twentieth century, a national, uninterrupted system of highways was merely a dream. Early attempts to link areas of America by road were limited by the untamed natural landscape and very little government funding. Despite these obstacles, the National Road was built in 1815. At the time of its construction, it was the most ambitious road-building project ever undertaken in the U.S. It eventually extended from Cumberland, Maryland to St. Louis, Missouri and served as the great highway of Western migration. This road, however, fell into disrepair in 1841, when no federal funding was set aside to maintain it.

Advocates of good roads sought to devise routes to link the newly created small towns and create a federal highway commission. Property owners quickly realized that any town through which the sanctioned road passed was sure to prosper, and anyone who owned land along that route would have a captive audience. What were once livery stables or blacksmith shops and even private homes became souvenir stands, restaurants, automobile repair stations, and every type of roadside oasis for weary travelers.

By the early 1900s, there were about eight thousand automobiles in the United States. Almost all of these were concentrated in major cities and were owned by the wealthy for convenience and pleasure. However, pleasure driving was restricted by a host of state and local laws and ordinances. Some cities and villages required a "wheel tax"" for the privilege of driving on their streets. All of these obstacles, as well as the immense cost and difficulty of maintaining an automobile, placed a severe burden on the vehicle owner and limited most "casual" automotive travel to city driving. The cost plus the lack of good quality roads kept most people traveling by train or steamboat to visit tourist destinations.

In 1903, three successful transcontinental trips were made. Credit for the first goes to Dr. Nelson Jackson and Sewall Crocker, who drove a 20-horsepower Winton touring car from San Francisco to New York in forty-six days. They wisely decided to bypass the snowy Sierra Nevada and went north to Lakeview, Oregon, then across eastern Oregon to Idaho. It was still a story full of broken connecting rods, Italian workers pulling them out of Wyoming rivers, and mules pulling them out of Nebraska mud holes. Many people who these automobilists met had never seen a car before. The publicity generated by these early ventures gave an enormous boost to the public's idea that the automobile was a thing of the future and not just a novelty.

Even with the restrictions of poor roads, there was a new breed of Americans who were suddenly able to explore the newly opened American continent. These fearless early adventurers drove down the open road, taking little with them other than a crude map and a desire to investigate the still untamed wild frontiers. Fuel tanks thirsty for gasoline, radiators in need of water, and travelers in need of rest and food resulted in the first gas stations and food stands along what used to be the dirt roads of the early highway system. Many of these early travelers were women, who sought the freedom and adventure of the open road. They kept travel diaries and scrapbooks, collecting small trinkets and paper goods to record their courageous adventures. Some of these early travel diaries are now in museums.

The fear of breaking down on poor roads, possibly miles from any town without a hotel, led travelers to begin outfitting their vehicles with camping equipment. They fashioned large metal storage bins on the runners of their model T's and stored tents, chairs, and small stoves. Some automobile owners viewed themselves as pioneers and reveled in their ability to camp on the outskirts of towns or anywhere along the road. Besides the freedom, another benefit of camping along the side of the road was that it was inexpensive, and many vacation destinations offered no other type of accommodation.

The early auto campers often avoided hotels, even though most could easily afford the rates. When camping, the auto "gypsies" did not have to make reservations or eat at the times set by the hotel dining rooms. They did not have to tip, nor explain their sometimes disheveled appearance after a day on the road to a hotel lobby clerk. Camping provided ample room for a tourist's family in the small tent and easy access to his vehicle and supplies.

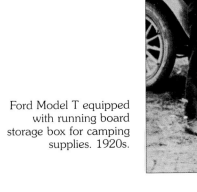

Ford Model T equipped with running board storage box for camping supplies. 1920s.

In the late 1910s, the idea of the "auto camp" was developed, as townspeople roped off spaces in which travelers could camp for the night. Camp supervisors—some of whom were employed by the various states—provided water, fuel, wood for camp stoves, privies or flush toilets, showers, and laundry facilities free of charge. This encouraged travelers to spend some time in the their town, bringing in much needed revenue. They also sold souvenirs to the tourists. The auto camping fad peaked between 1915 and 1922.

Auto Camp, Yellowstone Park, Wyoming. Circa 1918.

By the 1920s, the U.S. Department of Agriculture saw the need to connect the east and west coasts of the North American continent with a highway that could be traveled by automobile. Thus, America's most famous road was created in the late 1920s. Route 66 began in Chicago, Illinois, and wound its way through seven more states before ending in sunny Santa Monica, California. The eight states included in the route were Illinois, Missouri, Kansas, Oklahoma, Texas, New Mexico, Arizona, and California. At the time, approximately eight hundred miles were paved. The remaining road was dirt, gravel, brick, or wooden planks. It wasn't until 1937 that the road was finally paved along its full route.

Route 66 passed directly through the main streets of town after town, giving it the nickname of "Main Street of America." For many that lived near this historical road, the highway became their livelihood. Shops and other roadside attractions sprang up along the route, providing goods and services for thousands of tourists. Enthusiastic, brightly colored signs encouraged the weary traveler to stop, take photos, and, buy colorful souvenirs.

By the mid 1920s, many towns along the new transcontinental highways set up organized roadside camps to accommodate travelers who chose to spend the night nearby. There were now over sixteen million motor vehicles nationwide. More than three hundred cities had roadside camping facilities for motorists and more than one million people used them. Streets and highways were quickly built or modernized and a uniform numbering system for highways was introduced in 1925. By 1930, nearly twenty-seven million cars were registered.

Another tourist invention born out of necessity was the simple roadside cabin. These were often very simple structures, only four walls and a roof with outdoor restroom facilities. Thousands of cabin clusters were built along the highways by the 1930s, along with mom and pop restaurants that served box lunches and fried chicken for the road.

The Great Depression struck the tourist trade a serious blow. Expenditures for hotels, restaurants, vacation clothing, and travel supplies fell from $872 million in 1929 to $444 million in 1932. It was obvious to the businesses that catered to travelers that the ones who would stay in business during tough times would be those who could appeal to the smaller number of tourists on the road. Enterprising small businessmen started advertising their establishments using colorful language and outrageous claims of "The World's Largest," or "The One and Only." It was also during this time that roadside stands, newsstands, and diners started selling souvenir linens to the traveler. Barth and Dreyfuss produced most of the linens sold between the 1930s and 1950s. They produced the lines "Yucca Prints" and "Cactus Prints." These early souvenir linens were small, boldly colored maps, covered with colorful icons of the states' famous attractions and resort destinations. They were printed on an ecru colored canvas burlap material that the maker called "Cactus Cloth."

By the late1920s, roadside advertising had become a normal operating cost for businesses that catered to tourism. Fanciful buildings, signs, and colossal sculptures were a colorful feature of highway travel, culture, and commerce during the 1920s and 30s. Highly visible and usually humorous, these "roadside attractions" were designed to catch the eye of the passing motorist and entice potential customers. The 1920s and, in spite of the Great Depression, the 1930s, literally changed the American landscape.

Tourist's Crying Towel. 1950s. Fun graphics poking fun at the tourist. $30-$40.

Los Angeles Smog Towel. 1950s. Making fun of the poor air quality in Los Angeles, California. $15-$25.

By the end of World War II, the automobile was the dominant form of transportation and the highway became the central means of travel of all kinds. With the continued improvement of the interstate highway system and the phenomenal prosperity of the American economy in the mid-twentieth century—resulting in the ability of Americans to travel at will—fierce competition developed among roadside marketers to attract the attention of the thousands of suddenly affluent tourists.

Brilliant designers and craftsmen from the sign industry were more than happy to accommodate. Drawing from Art Deco and contemporary modern design, these advertising artists created advertising signs announcing roadside attractions, state and national parks, restaurants, and other tourist destinations. Built of steel and glass, thousands of these garish, yet beautiful, structures were erected from coast to coast. Many remain to this day, and have become precious collectibles in their own right.

Eventually, auto camps and cabin camps gave way to motor courts, in which all of the rooms were under a single roof. Motor courts offered additional amenities, such as adjoining restaurants, souvenir shops, and swimming pools. It was in these souvenir shops, as well as in train stations and newsstands, that most of the souvenir linens we find today were originally purchased.

West coast architect Arthur Heineman is credited with combining the words "motor" and "hotel" to create "motel," the name for the most popular destination of the American motorist in 1950s. The neon sign lit the way. In the 1940s and 1950s, most Americans who drove the highways preferred these new accommodations, which had emerged from the demand created by the boom in automobile travel.

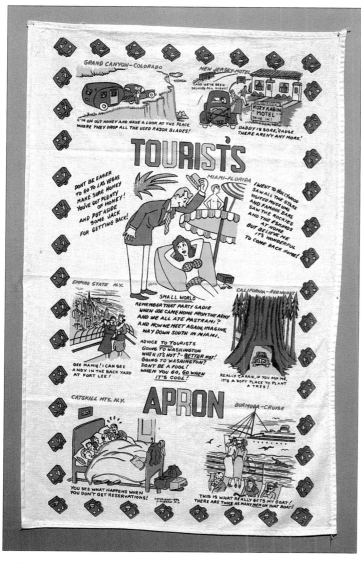

1940s Tourist's Apron towel. Why it says "apron," I don't know. Whimsical graphics. $20-$25.

1940s Alaska towel. Funny political reference to Stalin (the bear) and Russia. Souvenir for the soldiers stationed at the Alaska military bases. $30-$45.

After World War II, tourist attractions such as national parks, historic sights, and vacation resorts now had to compete with a variety of other tourist destinations, including theme parks, roadside attractions, and the rising numbers of ski parks and seaside resorts. Places such as Disneyland, which opened in Anaheim, California in 1955, epitomized a new form of tourist destination that catered predominately to amusement rather than cultural fulfillment or identity. In addition to Disneyland, new recreational and entertainment centers such as Aspen, Vail, and Las Vegas came to dominate the tourist industry. With these new tourist destinations now located in cities, a new type of souvenir linen was marketed and sold, one showing the tourist destination as well as the surrounding city or area. Disneyland, Atlantic City, and Las Vegas tablecloths, towels, scarves, and aprons were purchased by tourists as souvenirs to show to the folks back home.

Tourism, which prior to the war had focused on discovering and exploring the vast unknown America, had instead, become a quest for amusement and entertainment. Post war Americans were entertained by magazines like *American Tourist* and television shows depicting the "Wild West" and space explorations. Futuristic scenes and fantasy were some of the most popular themes of the tourist industry. This was reflected in the tablecloth designs of the late 1950s as cartoon figures and exaggerated graphics of whimsical tourist venues appeared on the souvenir linen.

The evolution of these tourist destinations is still well documented in the old roadside architecture along U.S. highways. Old billboards still advertise now defunct attractions. The remains of motels, auto cabins, and the shells of former gas stations litter the path of many two-lane highways, deserted of tourists. Formerly bustling main streets, which used to see visitors from all over America, today serve only their local community. And many small towns, now cut off from a major highway, are close cousins to ghost towns. What remains of these icons of the past are whimsical vintage souvenir linens, textile postcards from the America of our past that can still serve in our contemporary kitchens.

National Parks
and National Monuments

Some of the earliest tourist destinations were the national parks and monuments. The national park idea, the concept of large-scale natural preservation of wilderness areas for public enjoyment, has been credited to the artist George Catlin, best known for his paintings of American Indians. On a trip to the Dakota region in 1832, he worried about the destructive effects of America's westward expansion on Indian civilization, wildlife, and wilderness. He documented his experience and wrote in his journals that he hoped that these areas might be preserved for all to see.

While the early national parks were being established by The Forest Reserve Act of 1891, a separate movement arose to protect the prehistoric cliff dwellings, pueblo ruins, and early missions found by cowboys, army officers, ethnologists, and other explorers on the vast public lands of the Southwest. Efforts to secure protective legislation began among historically minded scientists and civic leaders in Boston and spread to similar circles in other cities during the 1880s and 1890s.

Comparable to the Forest Reserve Act of 1891, the Antiquities Act of 1906 was a blanket authority for presidents to proclaim and reserve "historic landmarks, historic and prehistoric structures, and other objects of historic or scientific interest" on lands owned or controlled by the United States, as "national monuments." It also prohibited the excavation or appropriation of antiquities on federal lands without permission from the department having jurisdiction. Shortly after the Antiquities act was passed, many of the historic landmarks we see today were officially preserved for future generations.

Chapter 2

State Souvenir Linens

Most of us have memories of family vacations, of traveling through the United states by car, stopping periodically at quirky tourist attractions. Many of us also purchased something to take home to remind us of the trip. One of these items might have been a souvenir tablecloth, towel, or scarf. Today, vintage souvenir linens are extremely collectible, increasing in value every year as more and more people are drawn to the charm and whimsy of these pieces from our past. Not only are these linens collectibles you can use, they also convey a real sense of nostalgia of days gone by, a gentle reminder of the United States of our childhoods and of the quaint roadside attractions and rural small towns that today are rapidly disappearing.

These wonderful collectibles are snapshots of our history as Americans, and of America's past, captured by enthusiastic textile designers on whimsically printed cloths. Collectors are attracted to the pleasing combination of strong graphics, bright colors, and the dizzying array of designs and textures. Many different styles of state and city souvenirs were produced for every state, so there are literally hundreds of possibilities to collect. One of the reasons state souvenir linens are increasing in value is that they are an example of a "cross collectible." Both the vintage printed tablecloth collector and the state souvenir collector share a love of these pieces of American memorabilia.

Although state souvenir tablecloths were produced as early as the 1920s, they rapidly increased in popularity as more and more Americans set out to discover the United States by car. This urge to travel was due to the combination of America's newfound wealth with the production of mass-produced, affordable automobiles. People then chose to travel by car on vacation, instead of taking the train or bus. Americans were eager to take to the road to discover America, buying souvenir linens from the states they visited. Amazingly, it is still possible to find examples of these souvenir linens with their original tags still attached, since many were put away in the linen drawer soon after the family returned from vacation. All states at one time sold souvenir tablecloths, aprons, and towels, although some examples are harder to find than others.

The earlier state tablecloths, from the 1920s, were small, usually 34" or 38", and not as detailed as the later ones. They were more often than not just one color and stamped with a simple one color border design. Most of these were souvenirs of national parks or monuments. During the 1930s and '40s, tablecloths and small towels continued to be popular souvenirs. By the late 1940s, most states had some type of souvenir linens to offer the tourist. As their popularity increased, tablecloths began to be produced utilizing more color combinations and in the larger sizes of 52" and 64", with coordinating napkins for use at the family kitchen table.

In the 1950s, many of the states hosted yearlong events honoring their statehood centennial celebration. Startex and Hardy Craft were two of the major manufacturers that produced "Centennial" souvenir tablecloths for such occasions. Even though these are more difficult to find, they are delightful snapshots of state history and are easy to date. There are also several examples of United States map tablecloths featuring all the states, although they can be difficult to find. These were popular souvenirs just after World War II, as a proud generation embraced their cultural identity and all things "American."

Rare Atlantic City Centennial tablecloth. Celebrates the city's 100th anniversary, 1854-1954. 49" x 48". $250-$300. *From the collection of Jorene Uluski.*

Most of the U.S. map tablecloths that you can find date between 1945 and 1955, just prior to the addition of Alaska and Hawaii as states.

The most highly sought after state tablecloths are those from states that were not as popular as tourist destinations. Souvenir linens from the states of Georgia, North and South Carolina, Alabama, Mississippi, and Tennessee can be the most difficult to find and can be valued as high as $575. California, Florida, New York, Alaska, Nevada, Hawaii, and Wyoming, as well as the states that Route 66 cut through, were the most popular destinations. These souvenir state tablecloths are easiest for the collector to acquire. Occasionally, you will find a Startex, Hardy Craft, or Simtex label on these tablecloths—demonstrating their immense popularity, as the large tablecloth manufacturers responded to the market demand for souvenir linens.

Souvenir tablecloths were also produced to showcase a specific popular tourist destination or a city. You can find tablecloths featuring "Lake Michigan," "Yellowstone Park," "Washington D.C." and "Los Angeles," just to name a few. These are a little harder to come by and are a delightful addition to your state souvenir tablecloth collection.

Alaska

Early Alaska 1942 tablecloth. Mentions the "New International Highway," which was built in 1942 to move troops and supplies during the war. The name was changed in 1945 to "Alaska Highway." Evidence of over dying yellow and blue to make green. 48" x 47". $55-$65.

Bold 1949 Alaska tablecloth. Depicts the Naval Operating Base in the Aleutian Islands, which operated from 1925-1949, and the Alaska Highway system that opened in 1949. 40" x 42". $50-$65.

Early one color 1940s tablecloth. 32" x 35". $30-$40.
From the collection of Erin Sherman.

Alaska "The 49th state" apron. Bold
graphics of the newest state in the Union.
Late 50s-early 60s. $15-$20.

ALASKA'S FLAG

Eight stars of gold on a field of blue—
Alaska's flag— May it mean to you
The blue of the sea, the evening sky
The mountain lakes   and flow'rs nearby.
The gold of the early sourdough's dreams.
The precious gold of the hills and streams
The brilliant stars in the northern sky
The "Bear"-the Dipper and shining high
The great North Star with its steady light,
Over Land and sea a beacon bright.
Alaska's flag-to Alaskans dear,
The simple flag of a last frontier.

Marie Drake

1950s Alaska tablecloth. Marie Drake wrote the words to the song "Alaska's Flag." The Territorial Legislature adopted "Alaska's Flag" as Alaska's official song in 1955, and Alaska became the last state entered in to the Union in 1959. 59" x 55". $45-$60

Alaska towel. Late 1950s. $10-$15.
From the collection of Jenny Kuller.

Alaska Territory tablecloth. 1955 (pre-statehood), depicting Marie Drake's song and the seal of the territory. Two color overprinting. 60" x 58". $45-$60.

Arizona

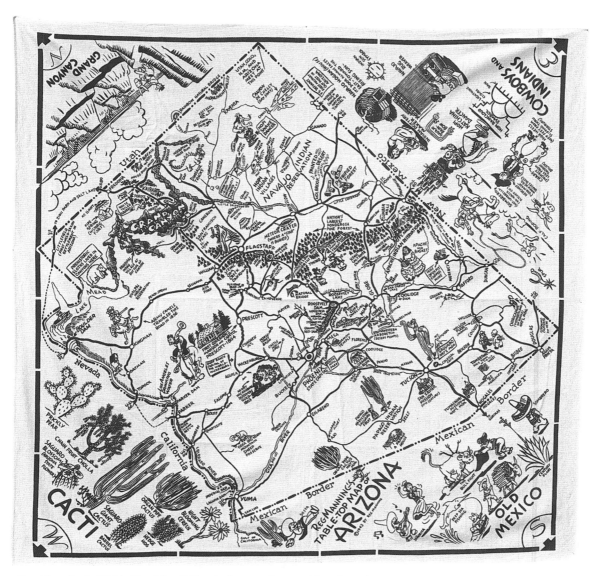

Reg Manning's "Table Top Map." Comical one color graphics of cowboys
and Indians. Dated with the copyright mark of 1943. 52" x 50". $150-$165.

Phoenix souvenir towel. 1970s. $8-$10.
From the collection of Erin Sherman.

Mint with tag, Cactus Cloth Arizona apron. Cowboys and Indians, bold color, and graphics. Still has the J.J. Newberry price tag of $1.00. $15-$20.

Close-up of the Cactus Cloth label.

Mint with tag, Cactus Cloth Arizona tablecloth. Great graphics of the old hotels and cabin camps help date this to the early 1940s. 50" x 52". $150-$165.

Kaibab National Forest tablecloth. Graphics of the
Grand Canyon auto cabin camp help date this to
the late 1930s. 49" x 50". $125-$150.

Arizona apron, 1960s. $10-$15.

Arizona tablecloth. Mid 1950s design
and graphics. 46" x 50". $50-$65.

1950s Arizona apron. Fun graphics. $10-$15.
From the collection of Jenny Kuller

Unusual brown and burgundy two color Arizona tablecloth. 46" x 50". $65-$80. *From the collection of Jenny Kuller.*

1940s Arizona tablecloth. Depicts Boulder dam, which changed its name to Hoover Dam in 1946. Dam and copper mines graphics help date this to between 1935 and 1945. 39" x 48". $55-$75.

Late 1930s Arizona tablecloth. Depicts Lowell Observatory, which was a popular tourist destination after it was credited with discovering Pluto in 1930. 49" x 50". $50-$65.

Bold 1960s California tablecloth. Depicts Knotts Berry Farm and other '60s popular tourist attractions. 49" x 50". $60-$75.

Early 1950s California tablecloth. Fanciful cartoon graphics of people enjoying
California tourist attractions. Note the naked mermaid and fisherman off the coast.
Also makes fun of the name change to Hoover dam. 50" x 50". $75-$90.

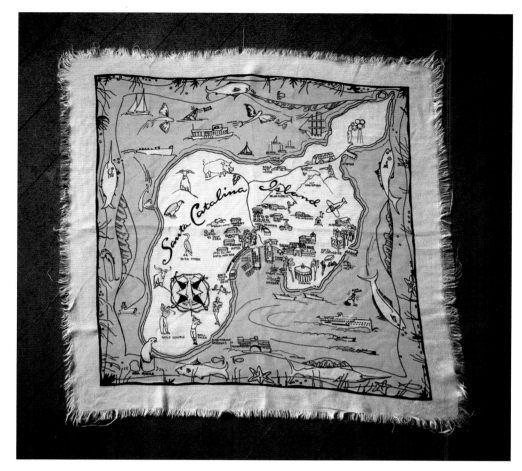

Santa Catalina Island breakfast cloth. This island was a popular tourist destination in the 1940s and frequent movie production location. 30" x 30". $55-$60.

Rare 1950 Centennial celebration California tablecloth. Only produced for one year to commemorate the states 100th anniversary 1850-1950. 55" x 50". $225-$250.

1950s California tablecloth. Depicts the famous cities and tourist attractions of California. Was offered in several different pastel colors with coordinating napkins. 50" x 48". $55-$75.

Close-up of the relief map graphics.

Mint with tag California tablecloth. Produced by "Yucca Prints" in the mid 1940s. 40" x 39". $75-$95.

1960s Knotts Berry Farm Tablecloth. Showcases the "old west" and "ghost town" early themes of the amusement park. 48" x 49". $75-$90.

1940s California apron. Fun graphics of California tourist destinations. $15-$20.

Margaret Newport signature.

Early 1940s darling California tablecloth designed and signed by "Margaret Newport." Depicts Boulder dam, which operated under that name from 1933-1945. After 1946 the name was changed to Hoover dam. 50" x 49". $55-$75.

Close-up of the Route 66 graphics.

Early 1940s one color stamped California tablecloth. Graphics of the "new" highway system including Route 66. 31" x 28". $55-$75.
From the collection of Jenny Kuller

Early 1940s California tablecloth. Depicts Boulder Dam and early Las Vegas graphics. 51" x 42." $55-$75. *From the collection of Erin Sherman.*

1950s California tablecloth. Whimsical primary colored graphics. Many souvenir manufacturers re-used their graphics for many years—note many of the same graphics as the 1950s California towel at right, including the Reno divorce graphic. 34" x 30". $45-$60.

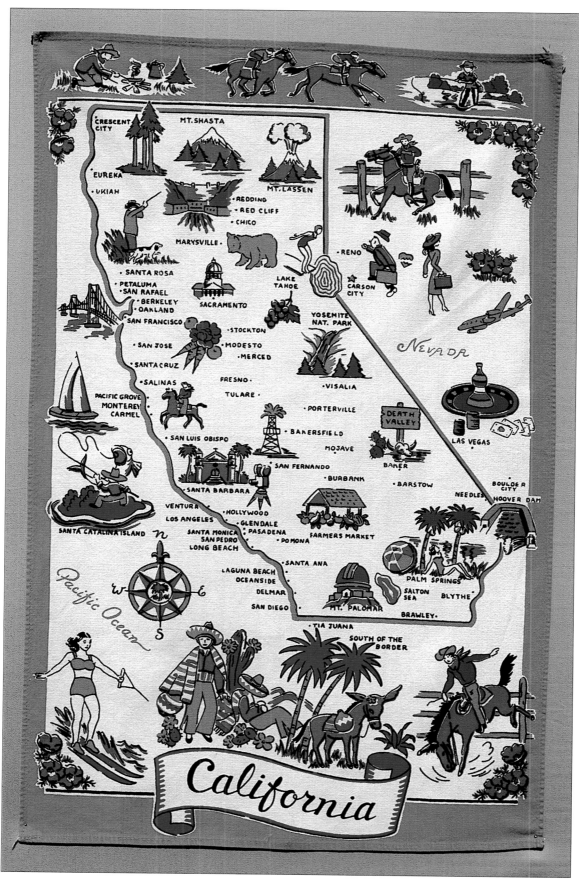

1950s California towel. Fun graphics…I love the Reno "divorce" graphics of the man running for his life and the woman marching away with her head held high. $15-$25.

Disneyland souvenir tablecloth, offered just after the park
opened in 1955. The graphics used on this cloth were the
concept sketches for the park, which were slightly different from
what was actually built. 46" x 49". $125-$150.

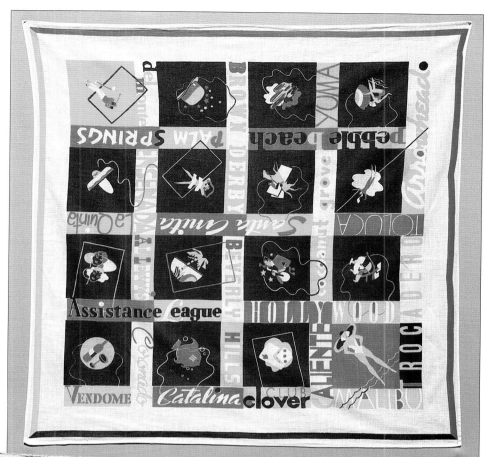

Unusual California scarf. Lists many of the 1940s and 1950s famous nightclubs and hot spots—most are now long gone. 29" x 29". $35-$45.

1940s California tablecloth. Depicts playful cartoon characters enjoying the tourist spots. The border graphics have a Mexican influence. Boulder Dam helps date this to between 1940-1946. 50" x 50". $65-$80.

1950s California tablecloth. Graphics used are more suggestive; the mermaid is topless and the Mexican dancer is shapelier than on earlier 1940s cloths. Hoover Dam reference helps date this to after 1948. 50" x 49". $150-$175.

World War II era southern California tablecloth. Shows the location of all the military bases in Southern California. Note the graphic in the corner: "Nevada— noted for divorces." Dates from between 1940-1945. 40" x 38". $75-$90.

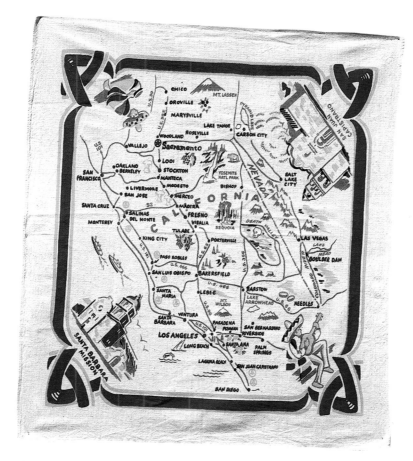

1950s California "Missions" tablecloth. All the locations of the early California missions are noted with yellow bell graphics. This tablecloth was sold in the mission gift shops. 38" x 35". $40-$60.

Mint with tag "Cactus Cloth" California tablecloth. Bold early 1950s graphics. Cactus Cloth prints were sold at newsstands and train stations. This one depicts March field, which was the strategic Air Command Center from 1949-1953. No other military bases are shown. 40" x 38". $75-$90.

Close-up of the Cactus Cloth tag. Produced by Barth and Dreyfuss, which also produced the "Yucca Prints" line of souvenir linens.

1960s California souvenir apron. Showcases Knotts Berry Farm and other points of interest, including Marineland, which operated from the 1950s-1970s. $25-$30.

Close-up of the "Sayers" copyright mark.

1930s California tablecloth. Over printed with early '30s moss green. Marked with a copyright "Sayers" in the corner. 60" x 49". $75-$95.

1930s R.A. McFarland tablecloth. Mint with tag, this is a rare tablecloth produced only for a few years between 1934-1939. Depicts unusual reference to "General Grant National Park." A small portion of what is now Kings Canyon was originally set aside in 1890 as General Grant National Park. In 1940, General Grant was absorbed into the new and larger Kings Canyon National Park. 49" x 50". $225-$275.

1972 California tablecloth. Dated with the original "ABC 1972 Long Beach" sticker. This was sold in small gift shops in Los Angeles and was locally produced. Great graphics of Disneyland, Knotts, and Marineland, which went out of business in the late 1970s. 38" x 38". $45-$60.

1960s California tablecloth. This one has many of the cities misspelled; for instance, "San Francisco" is misspelled "Sanfransisco" and "Mt St. Helen's" is "Mt St. Helena." Most likely an import from either Japan or China. 50" x 49". $60-$90.

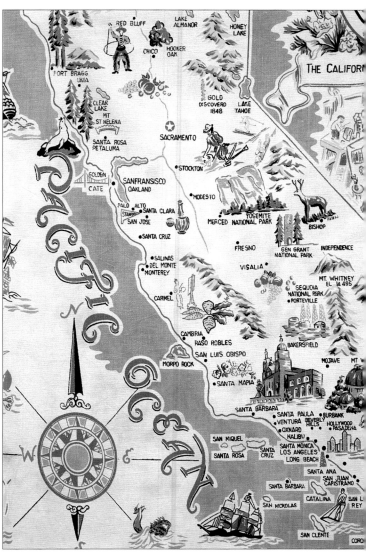

Close-up of the tablecloth—note the misspellings.

1950s San Francisco apron. Fun graphics of all the tourist spots including "Top of the Mark," located at the top of the Mark Hopkins Hotel. The hotel was named after Mark Hopkins, founder of the Central Pacific Railroad. In 1939, its 19th floor penthouse was converted into "Top of the Mark," a glass-walled cocktail lounge with a 360-degree view of the city below. $35-$50.

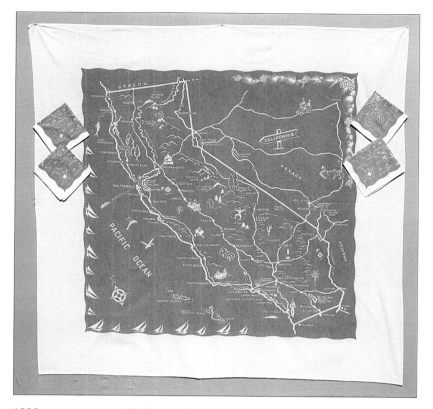

1930s reverse printed California tablecloth. This one highlights
the newly created highway system, including the famous "Route
66." Came with matching napkins. 56" x 50" $150-$175.

1960s plastic BBQ
California tablecloth.
Great graphics over
printed on a thick
plastic. 56" x 50".
$50-$75

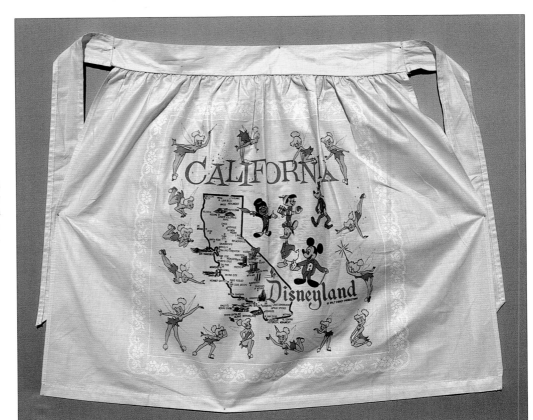

1960s Disneyland child's apron. Great Disney characters and a California state map. $40-$55.

1950s Yosemite National Park souvenir tablecloth. Depicts "Camp Curry" and the famous "Firefall" that thrilled tourists from 1908-1967. One of the more famous trees in the grove was the Wawona Tunnel Tree, a 234-foot-tall giant with a tunnel about 8 feet wide, 9 feet high, and 26 feet long. The Yosemite Stage and Turnpike Company paid about $75 in the early 1880s to have the tunnel cut big enough to drive wagons and, later, cars through. The Tunnel Tree was actually still alive and growing when heavy snow in its upper branches toppled it in the mid 1960s. 40" x 40". $200-$225.

1960s California apron. Amusing graphics, I love the cartoon Navy man enjoying the sites of Catalina Island. $30-$45.

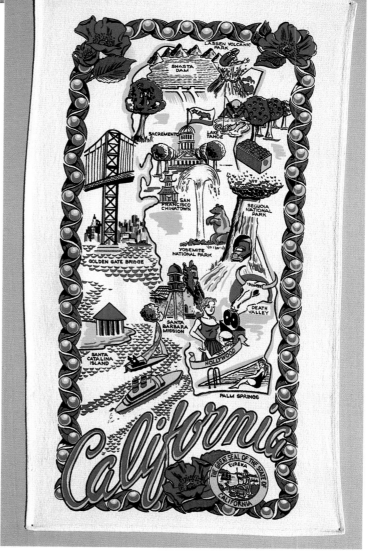

1950s California towel. Bold splashes of tourist destinations across the state, including Shasta Dam, Hollywood, and Catalina Island. $35-$45.

1940s "Land of Sunshine and Unusual Weather" tablecloth. One color graphics of the state, including a reference to the "1939 San Francisco Exposition." 52" x 49". $175-$190.

Close-up of the small reference to the "1939 San Francisco Exposition."

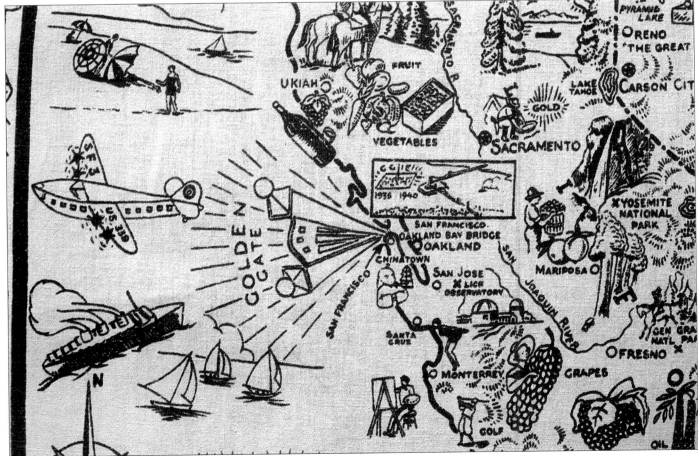

Colorado

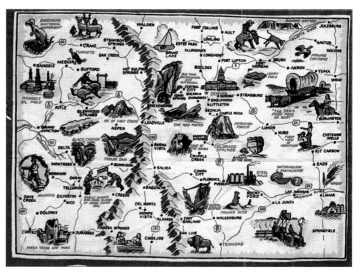

Close-up of the map graphics.

"Yucca Prints" mint with tag Colorado tablecloth. Bold colored graphics depict the beauty and grandeur of the state known for its dinosaur monuments and outdoor activities. No military bases are shown so it's pre-WWII 1940s. 50" x 50". $150-$175.

Close-up of the Yucca Prints tag. This line was manufactured by Barth and Dreyfuss of California.

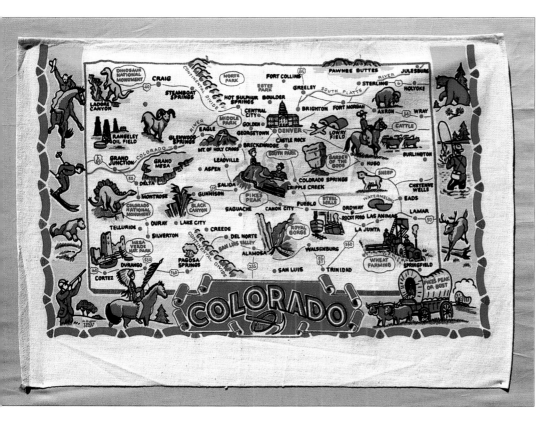

Colorado towel. Wonderfully bold and very colorful graphics. 1940s. 29" x 17". $25-$40.

Unusual 1930s Colorado tablecloth. Edged in blue columbine, the state flower, with early '30s moss green. It is interesting to note that it contains the statement "Mount Evans highest peak in the U.S." this mountain is now number 14 in Colorado and number 17 in the United States. 60" x 50". $ 50-$75.

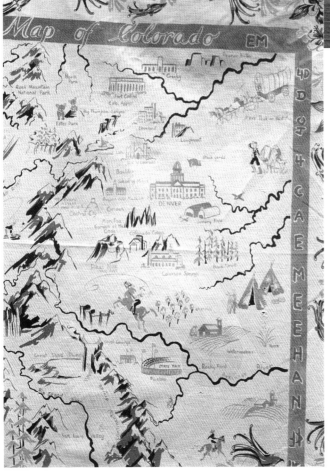

Close up of the 1930s Colorado tablecloth graphics.

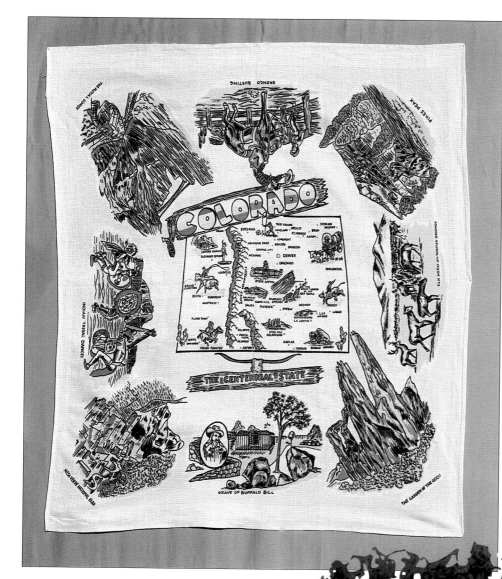

1950s Colorado tablecloth. No depiction of any of the state parks or national monuments. Large graphics of other Colorado tourist destinations, including the "Grave of Buffalo Bill." 47" x 42". $95-125.

1920s pillow cover souvenir. Pillow covers were very popular in the 1920s and 1930s—they were small and easy to carry. This one is hand blocked with very early graphics. $40-$65.

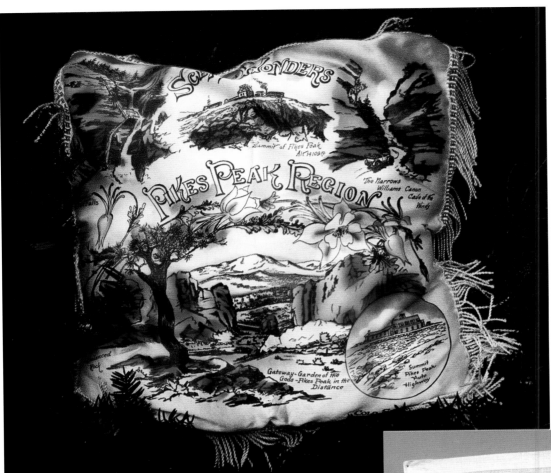

Wonderful 1920s "Pikes Peak" pillow cover. Named for Lt. Zebulon Pike, an explorer who was sent to map the new area acquired as the "Louisiana Purchase." In 1858, gold fever sent fortune seekers to the region, establishing many current towns like Cripple Creek and Victor. Shortly after the gold had panned out, General William J. Palmer arrived in the Pikes Peak region. His vision was one that would assure the quality of life of its residents while at the same time setting aside large sections of land for the establishment of parks. In the late 1930s, Spencer Penrose and Charles Tutt donated land for community use, built the Pikes Peak and Cheyenne Mountain Highways, and established the Cheyenne Mountain Zoo, Will Rogers Shrine, and the Broadmoor Hotel. $40-$55.

Colorado Centennial calendar towel. Celebrates the 100th year anniversary of statehood. $30-$45.

1920s "Seven Falls" Colorado Springs apron. Mentions "Helen Hunt's Grave." Helen Hunt Jackson's compassion for others, heightened by her own life's sadness after losing her sons and husband, eventually led her to become a very vocal critic of the unjust treatment of American Indians. In 1881 and 1882, she wrote a controversial book entitled *A Century of Dishonor* and spent five months in southern California documenting the mistreatment of American Indians in the old Spanish missions of the area. Two years later, she wrote the novel *Ramona*, a poignant love story about two mission Indians. Historians credit these two books with calling national attention to the plight of American Indians. $45-$60.

1930s Colorado tablecloth. Bold two color blue overprinting. Edge graphics show Colorado industries, including "Beets Sugar factory" and "Helium factory," two large industries in the '20s and '30s. I love the mountain climbers wearing cowboy hats. 51" x 50". $150-$200.

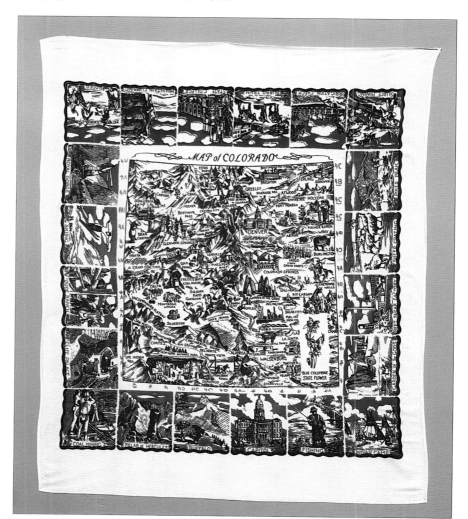

1940s mint Colorado tablecloth, produced by Davisco. This tablecloth
highlights the cantaloupe industry and steel mills. 39" x 38". $150-$175.

Connecticut

Ted Hilton Connecticut souvenir tablecloth. Depicts "Ted Hiltons" resort in Connecticut. Ted Hilton drove a taxi for a living in the 1930s. After taking groups of people from Hartford to resorts in Moodus, he decided that he wanted to run his own country resort and bought Elm Camp in the mid 1930s. It was most popular in the 1940s and 1950s. In each corner is a unique scene with the name of a different "Hilton" family member. 50" x 47". $75-$95.

Florida

Late 1950s Florida tablecloth, produced by "Vacationland of Miami." Depicts the Pensacola Naval Air Training Station, which operated in 1948; it then became the Naval Education and Training headquarters in 1971. Between 1918 and 1946 this site was a Navy Air station. 72" x 50". $75-$100.

Mint Belcrest 1970s Florida souvenir tablecloth. Depicts local Florida attractions including Walt Disney World, which opened in 1971. 54" x 54". $60-$90.

Close-up of the Belcrest label.

Close-up of the tag.

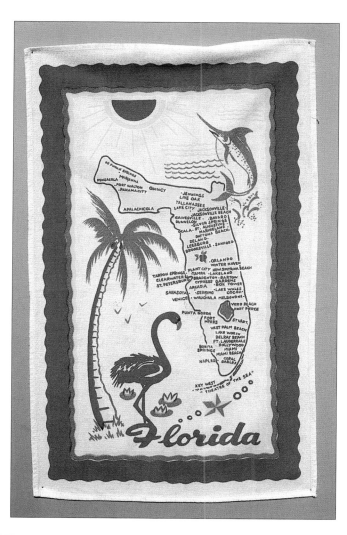

1930s Florida towel—note that not many cities are shown on the southern tip of Florida. In the 1930s it was still swampland. Florida didn't become a popular tourist destination until after World War II, when groups of enterprising builders filled the swamps and built large resorts. $35-$50.

1930s Florida souvenir tablecloth with matching napkins. Great late 1930s graphics on a small breakfast cloth. 32" x 30". $75-$150.

Late 1950s Florida tablecloth, produced by "Sherry of Miami." Depicts the Ringling Art Museum donated by P.T. Barnum's son just after his death in 1931, and the single span Sunshine Skyway that opened in 1954. A second parallel span to the bridge was completed in 1971. 60" x 50". $60-$75.

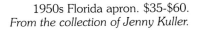

1950s Florida apron. $35-$60.
From the collection of Jenny Kuller.

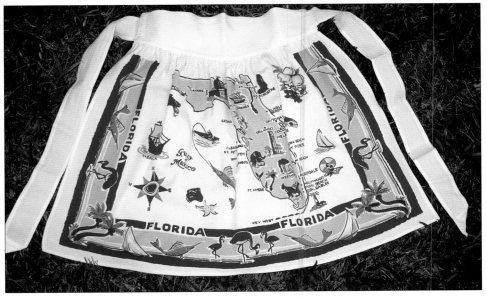

Late 1940s Florida towel. Over printed blues,
moss green, and maroon. $35-$50.

1950s Florida tablecloth, produced by "Sherry Manufacturing
Company." Depicts a dude ranch, which was a popular 1950s
resort destination. 54" x 54". $75-$125.

Close-up of the "Sherry" tag.

Close-up of the map detail.

Early 1940s Florida souvenir tablecloth. Fun cartoon graphics and details. 50"x 48" $100-$125.

Marked in the corner is "pat pending 1036352," which was applied for in 1935.

1960s Florida souvenir hanky. $15-$25.

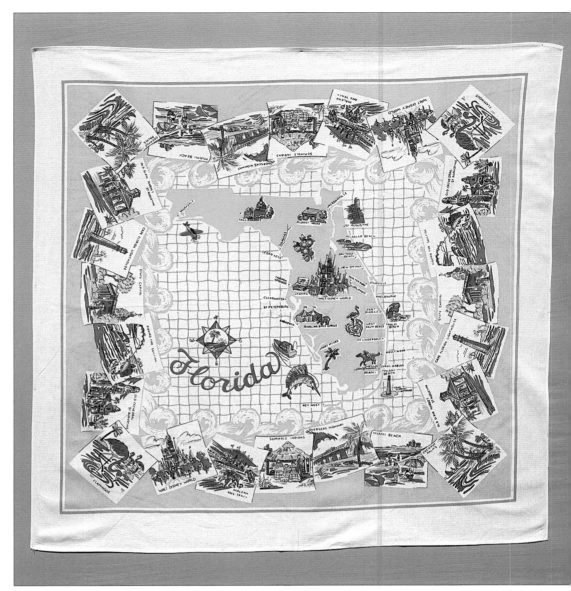

1970s Florida souvenir tablecloth. Highlights many of the popular tourist destinations, including Walt Disney World. 60" x 50". $50-$75.

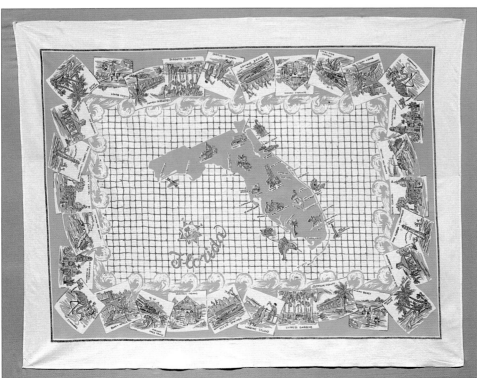

1960s Florida souvenir tablecloth. Exactly the same as the 1970s tablecloth except "Marine Studios" is high-lighted—no Disney World. 60" x 50". $60-$75.

Over printed 1940s Florida tablecloth. Interesting use of yellow in the palm trees. 50" x 50". $100-$125.

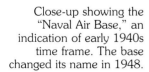

Close-up showing the "Naval Air Base," an indication of early 1940s time frame. The base changed its name in 1948.

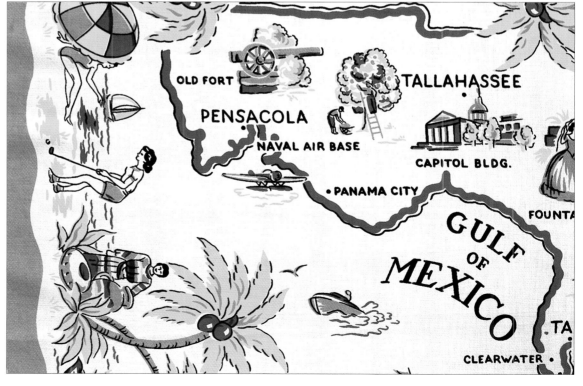

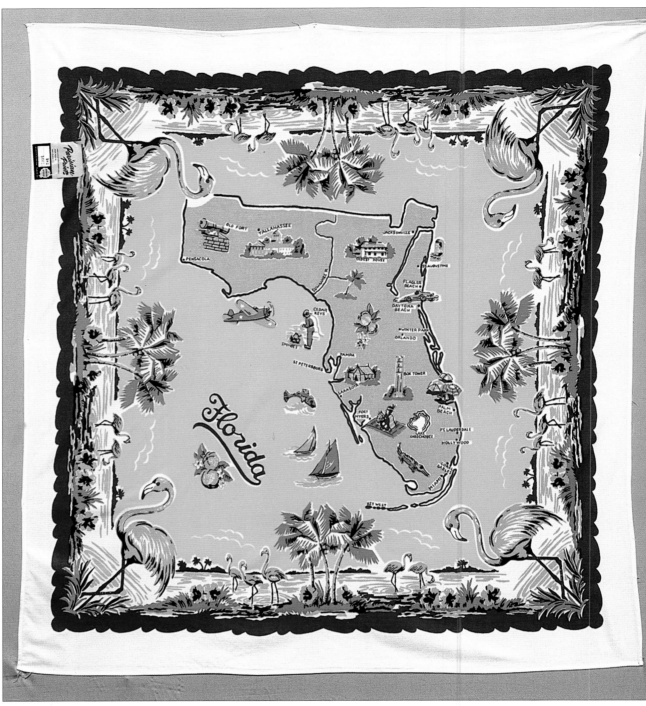

Mint 1950s Florida tablecloth. Incredible color combinations and wonderful flamingo edging. Mint with the original "Parisian Prints" label. 54" x 54". $225-$300. *From the collection of Linda Marrone.*

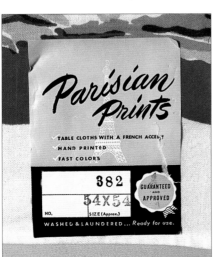

Close-up of the Parisian Prints label.

Fun 1950s Florida tablecloth. Flamingos and Southern Belles
grace the edge of this boldly printed cloth. 50" x 49". $150-$175.

1950s Hawaiian Islands tablecloth. Bold "pre-statehood" graphics of all the islands. Hawaii became a state in 1959. 39" x 35". $75-$90.

Late 1940s tablecloth designed by Connie Hilson for "Styled by Dervan." Rare pattern that depicts the path the Japanese planes took when they attacked Pearl Harbor from the North. 38" x 40". $125-$150.

Hawaiian Hula tablecloth. Sold to tourists in the 1950s. 50" x 49". $60-$75. There is also an exact reproduction of this tablecloth on the market today. It's 60" x 60" and has a sewn-in Moda tag.

1950s souvenir tablecloth. Depicts the military bases and local tourist hot spots of the 1950s. Most are long gone. 39" x 36". $55-$75.

1960s Hawaiian Island U.S.A. table-cloth. Dates to after Hawaii became a state in 1959. The outside floral pattern was made first, then the center panel was screen printed with multiple colors. 40" x 40". $40-$60.

1960s Oahu souvenir tablecloth. Makes reference to statehood so it's post 1959. Screen printed on heavy burlap. Fun colorful graphics. 32" x 30". $50-$75.

Hawaiian Hula girl tablecloth. Tourists could buy the hula girl tablecloth and stamp the details themselves, so many different variations of this tablecloth can be found on the market. 49" x 50". $60-$75.

1950s Aloha Tower Oahu souvenir. The Aloha Tower was constructed in 1926 at the Honolulu Harbor to create a lasting impression for boat passengers as they arrived and departed the islands, since visitors arrived at that time to Hawaii only by sea. This tablecloth was sold at souvenir stands greeting the arriving passengers. 49" x 40". $175-$190.

Illinois

1960s pink Chicago souvenir apron. Wonderful full color graphics. $20-$30.

1960s Chicago "The Windy City" scarf. 29" x 27". $40-$50.

1960s Indiana "Hoosier State" scarf. 29" x 28". $40-$50.

Kansas

Mint Kansas souvenir tablecloth. Cactus cloth line, depicts "Knute Rockne Memorial site" where in 1931 he and seven others were killed in a small plane crash. Also notes the "Home of Eisenhower" but not "President Eisenhower," so we can date this to between 1932-1945. 45" x 46". $150-$175.

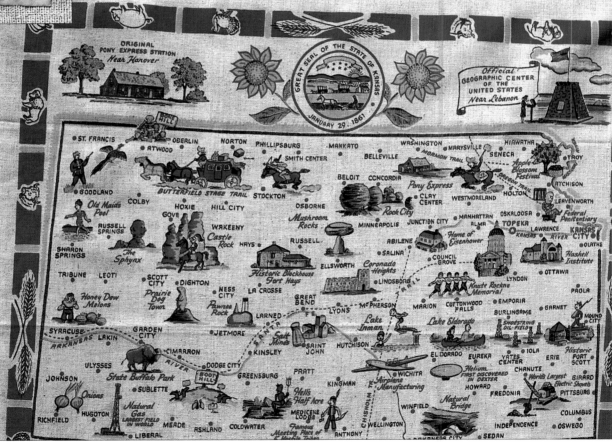

Close-up of the Cactus Cloth tag.

Detail of the bold graphics.

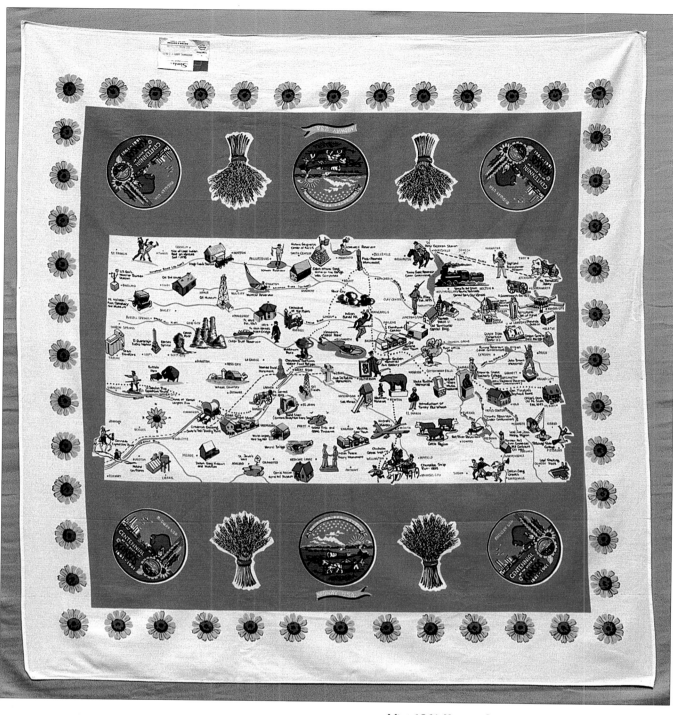

Mint 1961 Kansas Centennial souvenir tablecloth, produced by Simtex. Wonderful colorful graphics and fun history facts plus a great snapshot of life in Kansas in the 1960s. 52" x 52". $75-$100.

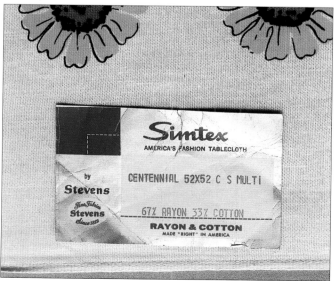

Close-up of the Simtex tag.

Kentucky "The Bluegrass State" 1940s pillow cover. $18-$25.

Kentucky souvenir towel. Produced by Kay Dee, 1970s. $10-$18.

Louisiana

Louisiana "New Orleans" tablecloth. 1930s graphics of old cars decorated for Mardi Gras and leather padded football players. 50" x 46". $75-90.

1960s New Orleans towel. French market graphics. $15-$25.

New Orleans souvenir apron. 1950s graphics depicting New Orleans as a "party town." $15-$25.

1940s New Orleans "The World's Most Interesting City" souvenir tablecloth. Depicts all the tourist destinations with an emphasis on historic architecture. $75-$90.

Close-up of the wonderful details.

1956 New Orleans souvenir towel. $15-$30.
From the collection of Jenny Kuller.

1940s New Orleans souvenir
towel. This towel coordinated
with a matching tablecloth of
the same design. $15-$20.

Fabulous 1960s New Orleans apron. Sheer apron with gold
accents and a great map of the city. $20-$50.

Maine

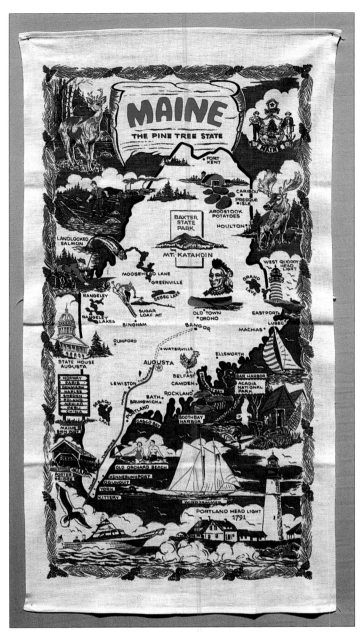

1960s Maine "The Pine Tree State" Kay Dee towel. Mentions Baxter State Park, which opened in 1952 after a generous donation of the land by P. Baxter, governor of the state from 1921-1931. $25-$40.

1950s Maine "America's Vacationland" towel. $35-$50.

1960s Maine "The Pine Tree State" Kay Dee towel in it's original packaging. $10-15.

Maine "The Pine Tree State" mint tablecloth. Produced by Cactus Cloth in the early 1950s. Mentions the "Lakewood Players 1901," a summer theater, and "Perry's Nut House." Both were a popular tourist destinations in the 1940s and 1950s. 39" x 38". $175-$225.

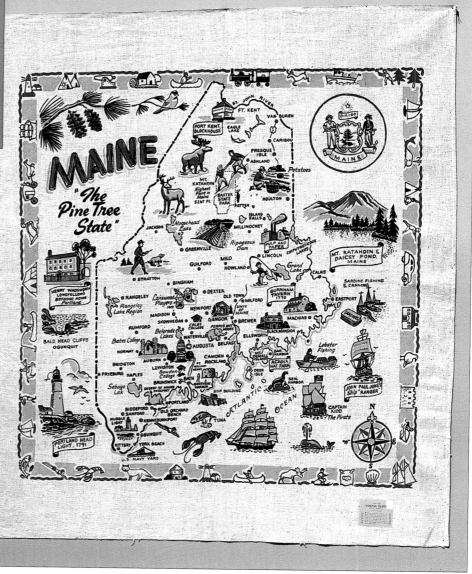

Massachusetts

Massachusetts tablecloth. This is a harder to find tablecloth with great early 1940s graphics. 32" x 30". $75-$125.

1950s Massachusetts towel. Depicts historical Massachusetts sites including the Mayflower landing at Plymouth Rock and Boston. Most likely a "Cactus Cloth" towel. $30-$50.

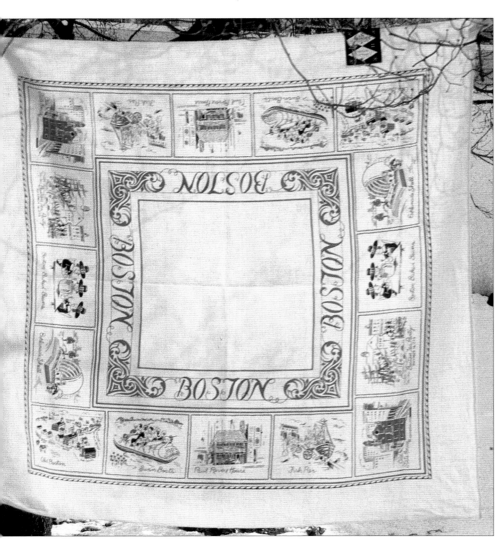

Falflax tag.

Mint "Falflax" 1950s Boston souvenir tablecloth. Rare tablecloth with great red and black cartoon graphics of historic Boston, including a reference to the "Swan Boats." These were created in 1877 and still continue to ferry tourists around the Boston Gardens lagoon. 50" x 50". $75-$150.

Close-up of the great cartoon graphics.

Michigan

Michigan tablecloth. 1950s graphics of the automobile industry and tourist attractions by the Great Lakes. 38" x 36". $75-$100.

1950s Michigan apron. Bold graphics. $35-$50.

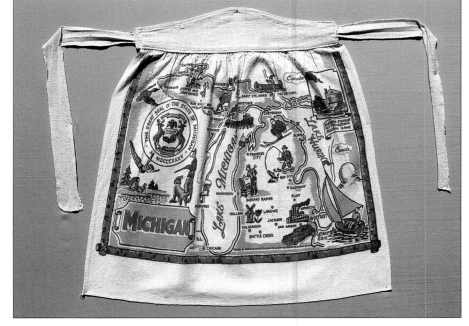

Michigan tablecloth. Shows the Grand Traverse region of Northern Michigan made
famous by its cherry orchards and lake resort destinations. 38" x 36". $50-$75.

1958 Minnesota Centennial tablecloth. Only available from "D&W Mail Order" for two years from 1957-1959. Fun graphics. Mint with the original label. 40" x 39". $100-$150.

Close-up of the label.

Minnesota "Land of 10,000 Lakes" tablecloth. 30" x 30". $75-$125.

1950s Minnesota towel. Great hunting and fishing graphics. $35-$50.

Early 1900s Rochester, Minnesota pillow cover. Mentions the "Worrel Hospital" founded by Dr. William Worrell Mayo in 1883. In 1914, it became the famous Mayo Clinic. Great piece of early Minnesota history. $55-$75.

Missouri

1950s Missouri "The Show Me State" souvenir
scarf. Bold colors and graphics. 29" x 27". $45-$60.

Missouri souvenir tablecloth. 1950s graphics of major Missouri industries including coal and steel mills and farms. These types of two color graphic maps were made for many Midwestern states by an unknown manufacturer. 49" x 50". $75-$95.

1950s Montana souvenir tablecloth. Bold cowboy and Indian graphics. $175-$200.

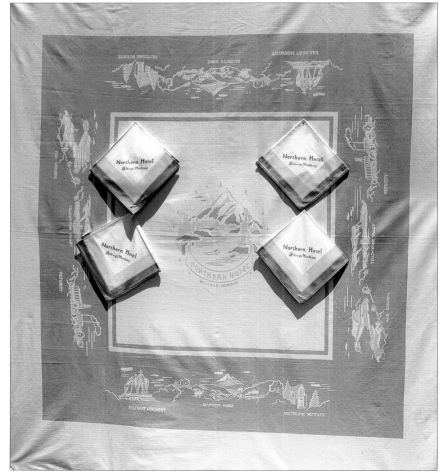

1950s Great Northern Hotel souvenir table-cloth and napkin set. On March 24, 1909, the Great Northern and Burlington railroad lines opened to the public. Hotels large and small sprouted at the heart of downtown Billings, Montana to serve travelers to the city. Most prominent were the Great Northern and the Grand Hotels. Begun in May 1902, the original 69-room Great Northern hotel opened in February 1904. It burned to the ground on September 11, 1940 but was rebuilt and still stands today. 60" x 60". $150-$175.

Montana souvenir tablecloth. Depicts the "Fort Peck Dam" which was completed in 1940. Also shows the Custer Battlefield National Cemetery, which was designated a National Cemetery in 1876 by executive order of President Grover Cleveland. In 1946, the site was designated a National Monument and renamed the Custer Battlefield National Monument. This name remained until December 1991 when it was changed to Little Bighorn Battlefield National Monument and Custer National Cemetery. Given this information, we can date this tablecloth to between 1940-1946. 50" x 50". $175-$200.

Nebraska

Nebraska "The Cornhusker State" 1932 tablecloth. Celebrates the building of the new state capital, which took ten years to design and build. It was completed in 1932 and was famous for its large sweeping art deco architecture and grand courtyards. 38" x 40". $200-$275.

1940s Nevada souvenir scarf. Great graphics of early Nevada before Las Vegas was a huge gambling tourist attraction. Shows the name change of Boulder Dam to Hoover Dam, which took place in 1946. 32" x 29". $55-$75.

1950s Las Vegas souvenir apron. Fabulous graphics of all the early big hotels in Vegas and the famous "Vegas Vic" icon, which was a huge neon figure that welcomed visitors to the city. $45-$65. *From the collection of Susan Lombardo.*

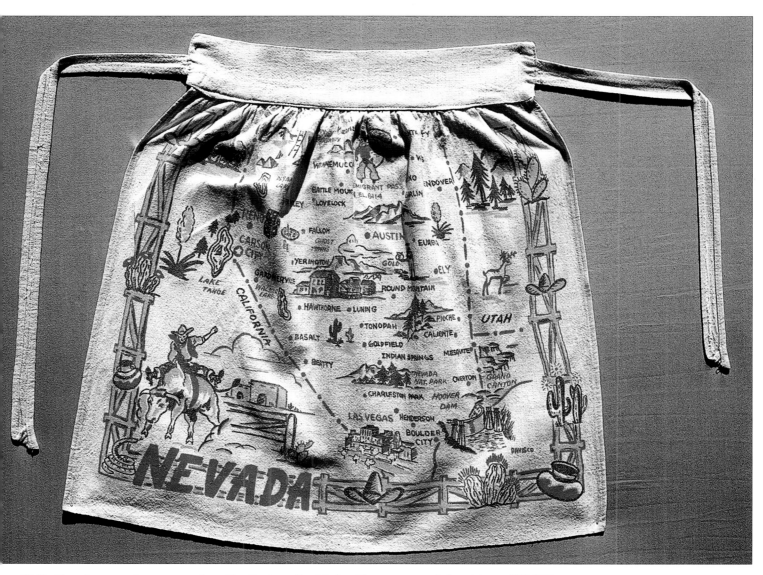

1940s Nevada souvenir apron, produced by Davisco. Depicts Las Vegas as a small desert town. $40-$60.

New Hampshire

Close-up of the Cactus Cloth label.

Mint Cactus Cloth New Hampshire tablecloth. Mentions the famous Ski mobile invented in the 1930s to lift skiers up the mountain and the now destroyed "Old Man of the Mountains" famous rock formation. No mention of any national parks, so we can date this to the early 1940s. 39" x 37". $150-$200.

Wonderful New Hampshire graphics.

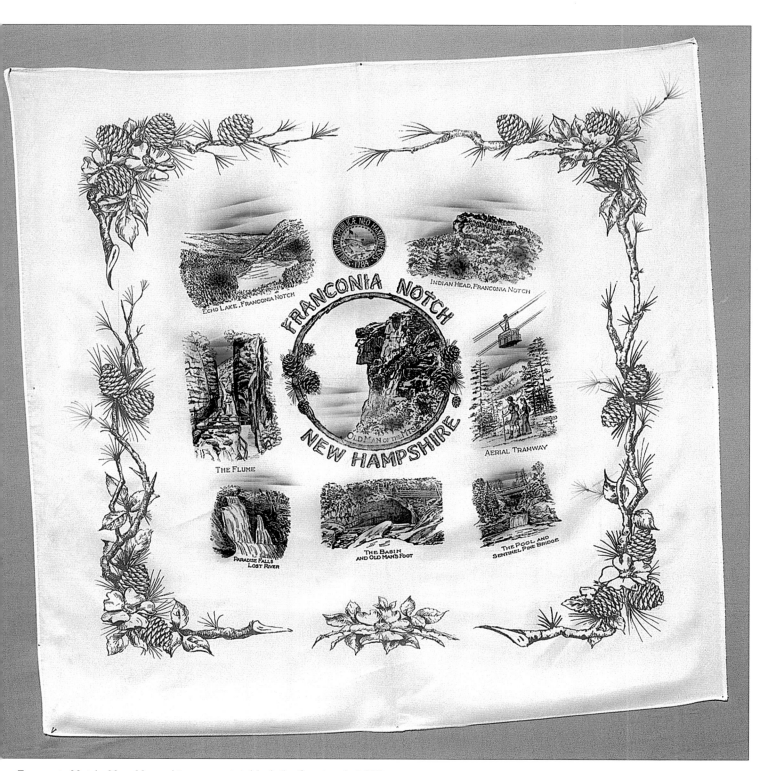

Franconia Notch, New Hampshire souvenir tablecloth. Great early 1920s
graphics of the area before it became a national park in 1928. Many of the areas
shown on this tablecloth were renamed in the 1940s. 34" x 30". $175-$225.

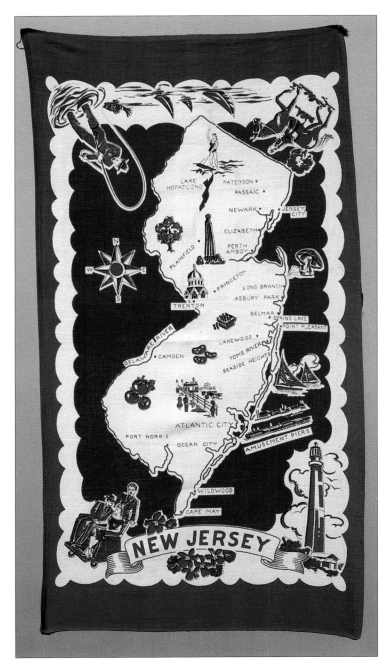

1940s New Jersey tablecloth. Fabulous early 1940s graphics including the Navy dirigible fleet that was stationed at Lakehurst from the early 1930s to 1945. Lakehurst was the site of the "Hindenburg" disaster of the 1930s. 49" x 47". $200-$250. *From the collection of Susan Lombardo.*

Wonderful 1930s New Jersey towel. Great graphics of Atlantic City and surrounding attractions. $25-$45.

1940s Atlantic City apron. Great graphics of the early Atlantic City coastline. $35-$50.

1940s Atlantic City souvenir tablecloth. Originally created in the 1850s as a genteel retreat for Philadelphia's upper crust, this seaside resort soon developed a madcap personality of its own, becoming one of America's most fabled cities. This tablecloth has great early Atlantic City "pre-casino" graphics, including the "Elephant Hotel," a building with an interesting history. Built in the late 1880s, "Lucy" (as the building was later known) was operated alternately as a tourist attraction, miniature hotel, private beach cottage, and tavern. In 1920, Lucy the Elephant tavern was forced to close by the passage of Prohibition. It immediately became a bar again upon repeal of Prohibition in 1933, but closed in the late 1950s. 48" x 47". $150-$225.

1940s New Jersey towel. Very early 1940s graphics of Atlantic City's steel pier and couples enjoying the sites. $45-$50.

Unusual Atlantic City souvenir tablecloth. A great 1950s rooster
themed tablecloth with "Atlantic City, N.J." stamped on each side.
52" x 50". $75-$100. *From the collection of Laura M. Schraeger.*

1940s New Mexico tablecloth. Proudly proclaims the "First atom bomb site" in 1945 and shows open pit copper mines. In 1947, a UFO was sited over Roswell, an account that was denied by the Air Force. Most 1950s souvenir textiles from New Mexico usually make some reference to the UFO incident. Since this one does not, we'd date it to the late 1940s. Produced by Yucca Prints. 49" x 47". $150-$175.

1940s New Mexico apron. Shows Route 66 going through the states and "Bottomless Lakes State Park," New Mexico's first state park in 1933. $40-$60.

1940s New Mexico "Land of Enchantment" tablecloth. Over printed design featuring whimsical cartoon graphics. Mentions several tourist destinations that were popular in the 1940s, including Carlsbad Caverns National Park. 56" x 52". $95-$125.

Close-up showing the whimsical cartoon graphics and bold colors that make this tablecloth one of my favorites.

New York

Rare 1930s New York tablecloth. This tablecloth was produced to commemorate the opening of the Empire State Building and was only sold for one year. Peach and blue over printed design featuring many of the large buildings and tourist destinations of the early 1930s. Includes Hell Gate Bridge, which opened in 1916 and was the longest steel-arch bridge in the world. It would hold that title until the Bayonne Bridge opened in 1931. 49" x 47". $250-$400.

Fun Niagara Falls souvenir tablecloth from 1941. Various scenes from the American side of the Falls, including the Peace Bridge which was constructed in 1927 and the "new" Rainbow Bridge which opened in 1941. 30" x 30". $55-$75.

1950s New York tablecloth. Great large scenes of supper clubs, Harlem, and other New York landmarks. 56" x 50". $175-$200.

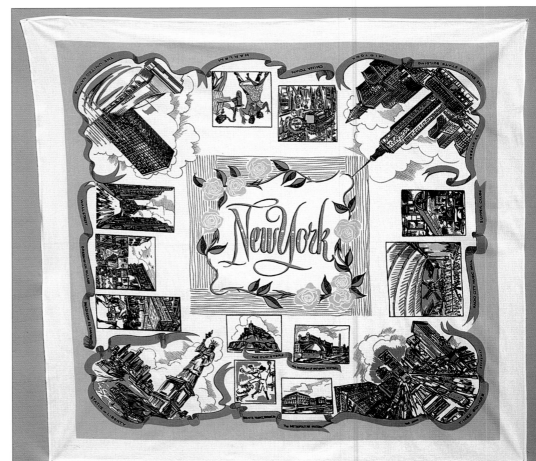

Same tablecloth with different color combination.

1950s New York tablecloth. Whimsical map and graphics of New York landmarks including the famous Rockefeller Center, America's largest privately owned business and amusement complex of the pre-war period. At first, the twelve-acre site was a failure and only attracted tenants after an outdoor skating rink was installed in 1941. 62" x 50". $200-$225.

1940s New York City tablecloth. Interesting reference to "Stuyvesant Town," a unique apartment complex that opened in 1947. Designed as an ideal middle-class community in Manhattan, Stuyvesant Town occupies eighteen square blocks; its brick buildings shut out the bustling city beyond the perimeter. Also depicts "La Guardia Field," which changed its name to La Guardia Airport in 1947. These two clues help date this piece to around 1947. 55" x 50". $250-$300.

Same tablecloth, different color combination.

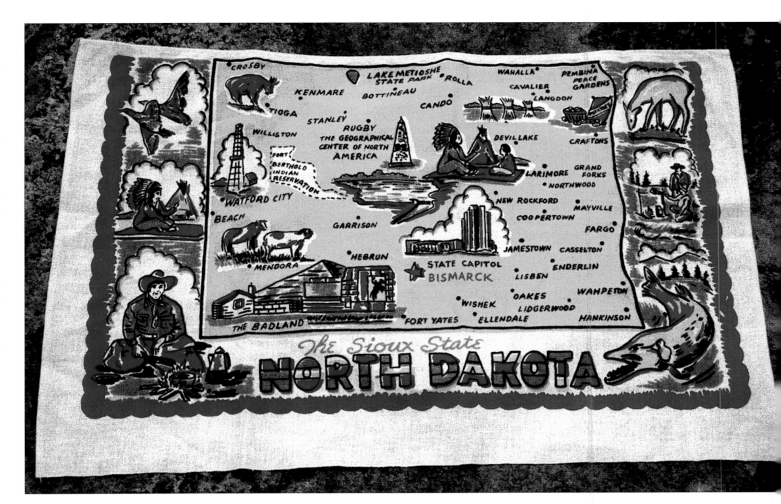

1950s North Dakota towel. Bold colors and fun graphics. $40-$55.

Ohio

Mid 1940s mint Ohio Yucca Prints souvenir tablecloth. Bold colors and wonderful graphics of many 1920s and '30s landmarks. It references "Art Pottery," which refers to clay deposits in the Zanesville, Roseville, and Crooksville area that encouraged settlers to manufacture ceramic products here early in the nineteenth century. The industry grew during the late nineteenth century as local potters turned to the production of highly decorative pieces. This "art pottery" remained popular until the 1920s. 50" x 50". $175-$225.

Close-up of the Yucca Prints tag.

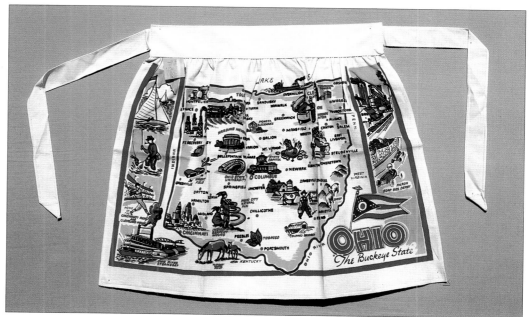

Ohio souvenir apron—matches the Yucca Prints tablecloth but is missing the references to "Edison Birthplace." Mint with the original Yucca Prints sewn in paper tag. $45-$60.

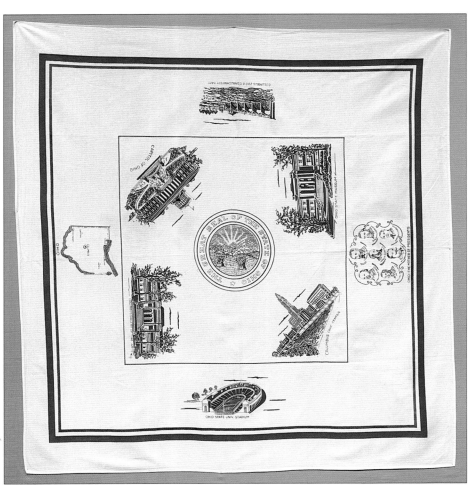

1930s Ohio souvenir tablecloth. Depicts many of the historic landmarks in Columbus, Ohio that were built in the 1920s. These include O'Shaughnessy Dam, completed in 1925, and Ohio Stadium, built in 1922 and listed in the National Registry of Historic Places. This was a set that came with four napkins. 48" x 47". $50-$60.

1930s Ohio souvenir tablecloth. Unusual color combinations and over printed design. 47" x 42". $95-$125.

Oklahoma

1940s Oklahoma souvenir scarf, "The Oil Well State." 29" x 27". $35-$50.

1950s Oklahoma souvenir scarf, "The Sooner State." 29" x 27". $25-$40.

1940s Oklahoma Souvenir tablecloth, "The Sooner State." Great
graphics including the "Grand River Dam," which opened in 1940 and
was quickly renamed the "Grand Lakes Dam." 49" x 47". $125-$140.

Pennsylvania

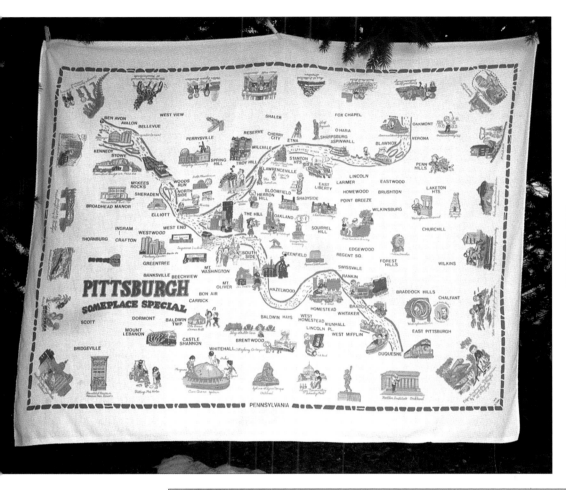

Pittsburgh souvenir tablecloth. Depicts fun cartoon characters and famous landmarks in the Pittsburgh, Pennsylvania area. Produced in 1980, it's signed in the corner "H.K. 2-1980." 70" x 50". $45-$65.

Pennsylvania souvenir towel. Showcases the "Bushkill Falls" and the "Delaware Water Gap," two the Keystone State's most famous scenic attractions. $20-$30.

1950s South Carolina "The Palmetto State"
souvenir scarf. 27" x 25". $30-$50.

South Dakota

Mount Rushmore souvenir tablecloth. One color graphics of the famous rock sculpture. Sculptor Gutzon Borglum began drilling into the 5,725-foot mountain in 1927. Creation of the monument took fourteen years and cost a mere $1 million, though it's now deemed priceless. 33" x 29". $50-$75.

South Dakota "The Sunshine State" souvenir tablecloth. Mentions many of the late 1930s landmarks, including the quirky "Corn Palace" and the "Badlands National Monument." It's missing many of the state parks and other national landmarks that were created in the mid 1940s so we can date this tablecloth to between 1939-1944. 42" x 39". $175-$225.

1950s South Dakota souvenir tablecloth. Features many of the national parks created just after the war, and the "Fort Randall Dam," which is misspelled on the tablecloth as "Fort Randell Dam." 46" x 40". $50-$65.

1950s South Dakota souvenir apron. Cowboys and Indians themed 1950s souvenir. $35-$50.

1960s Mount Rushmore souvenir towel. Wonderful facts and graphics. $25-$35.

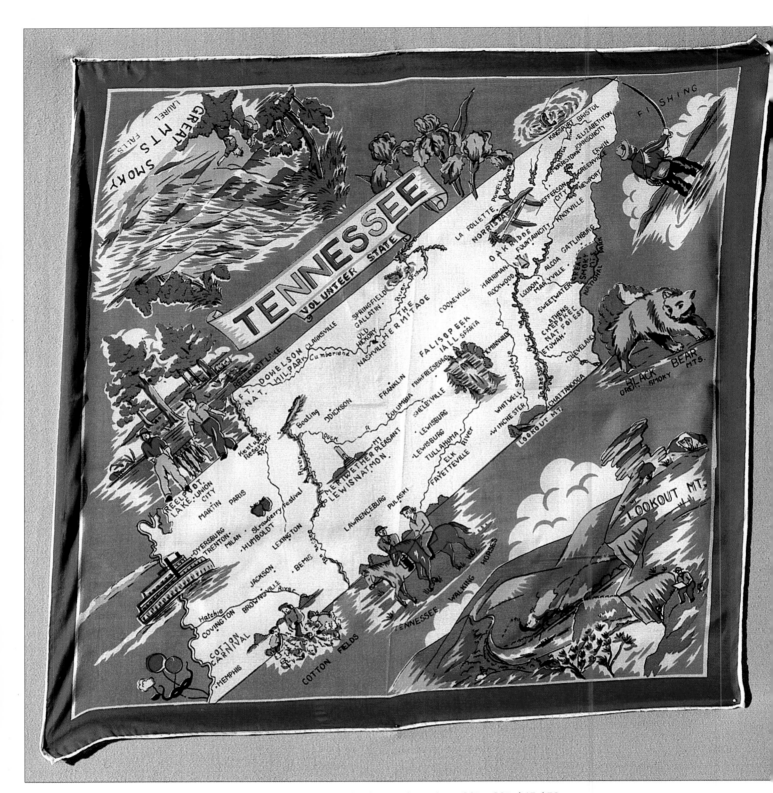

1960s Tennessee "The Volunteer State" souvenir scarf. Bold colors and graphics. 30" x 29". $45-$50.

Texas

Texas souvenir tablecloth. Mentions "Big Bend National Park," which was dedicated in 1944, and makes a rare reference to "U.S. Navy University of the Air" most likely a reference to "Randolph Field." No record of this location now exists. 45" x 40". $150-$175.

Close-up of the map details.

1940s Texas state tablecloth. Great cowboy graphics and only a vague reference to the oil wells that would become Texas's largest industry in the 1950s and 1960s. 47" x 46". $150-$175.

Rare Texas United States tablecloth from 1952. Wonderfully comical tablecloth that was produced by the Texas Textile Mills manufacturing group, with reference to "Map of the United States which is a part of Texas as seen from the Texas Textile Mills." Dated with a small reference to the "Cotton Bowl, Home of the Dallas Texans," a football team that only played for one year—1952. 56" x 50". $300-$450.

Early 1940s Texas "The Lone Star State" souvenir tablecloth. Over printed graphics, mentions "Randolph Field." After the Air Force became a separate service in 1947, Randolph Field was officially renamed Randolph Air Force Base. 52" x 50". $175-$200.

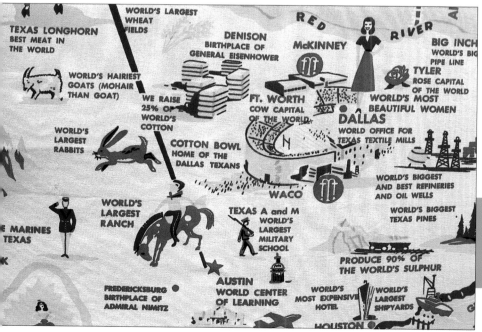

Details of the whimsical graphics.

Close-up of the comical reference.

Early 1940s Texas "One and Indivisible" tablecloth. World War II era tablecloth that depicts the military bases throughout Texas. This was sold on the military bases for the soldiers to send back home. 49" x 48". $200-$225.

Details of the crude humor.

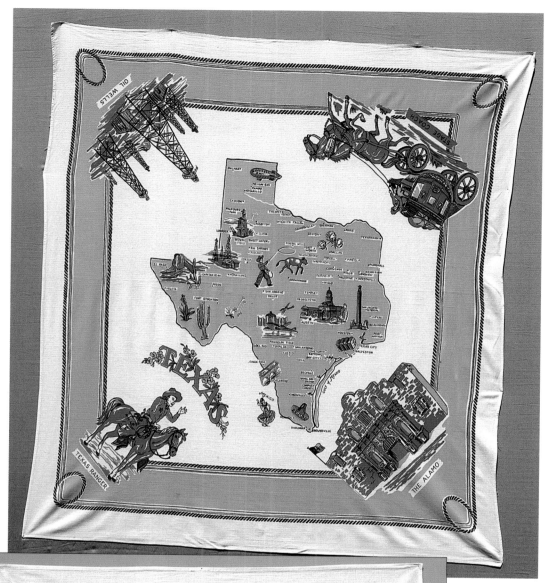

1940s Texas tablecloth.
This tablecloth has been
reproduced—the repro is
cotton with a wide sewn
hem and doesn't have
the gold embellishments.
50" x 50". $150-$175.

Early 1940s Texas tablecloth. Shows many
of the airfields that were combined into
"Randolph Field" in the early 1940s. 48" x
46". $100-$125.

Utah

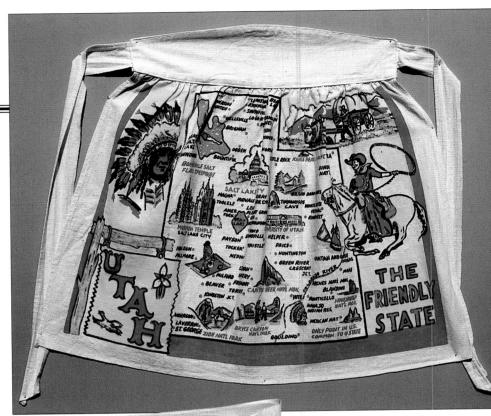

Utah "The Friendly State" apron.
1950s bold colorful graphics. $45-$60.

Utah tablecloth. One color
graphics depicting national
parks and landmarks in the
1930s. 50" x 50". $150-$175.

Vermont

1940s Vermont "The Green Mountain State" tablecloth. Great graphics including "Quechee Gorge," which was made into a state park in 1952. 39" x 38". $125-$150.

Virginia

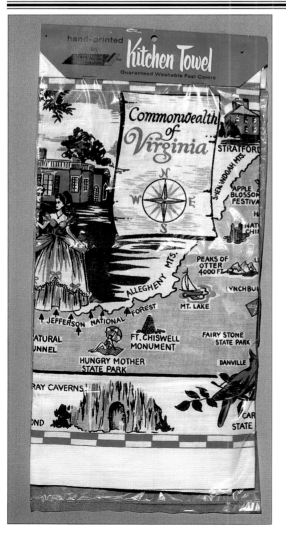

Close-up of the package.

Mint Virginia towel, produced by "Bestex." Mentions "Hungry Mother State Park." Legend has it that when the Native Americans destroyed several settlements on the New River south of the park, Molly Marley and her small child were among the survivors taken to the raiders' base north of the park. They eventually escaped. Molly finally collapsed, and her child wandered and found help. The only words the child could utter were "Hungry Mother." The search party arrived at the foot of the mountain to find the child's mother dead. Today that mountain is Molly's Knob, and the stream is Hungry Mother Creek. $25-$30.

Virginia "Old Dominion" scarf. Colorful graphics and lots of detail. 30" x 29". $60-$75.

Washington

Washington Oregon tablecloth. Fun cartoon graphics of early 1940s landmarks including "Bow Lake Airport," which only existed from 1941-1945. 39" x 38". $100-$125.

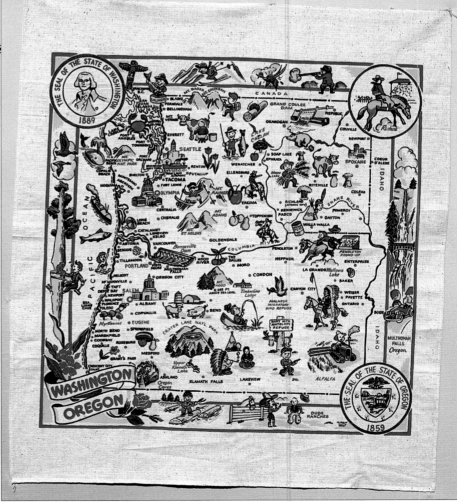

Close-up of the cartoon graphics.

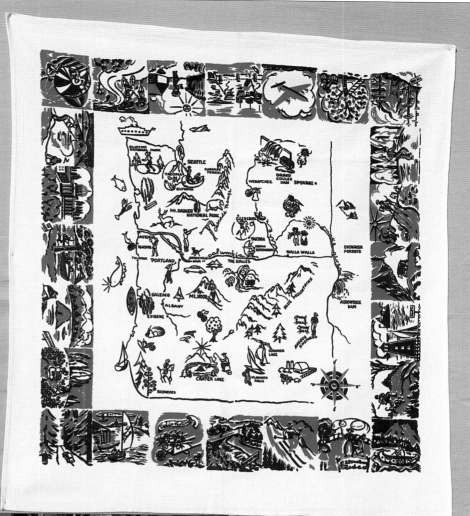

Washington state souvenir tablecloth. Over printed red and blue graphics, very simple design. Very early 1940s. 42" x 39" $75-$95.

1950s Washington state souvenir scarf. Bold colors and designs. 30" x 30". $50-$65.

Washington state souvenir tablecloth. Incredible colors and graphics. Depicts Washington landmarks like the Lake Washington pontoon bridge, which opened in 1940. 40" x 40". $95-$125.

Washington D.C.

Wonderful 1950s Washington D.C. souvenir tablecloth. Depicts one color graphics of the nation's most famous landmarks. 32" x 30". $50-$75.

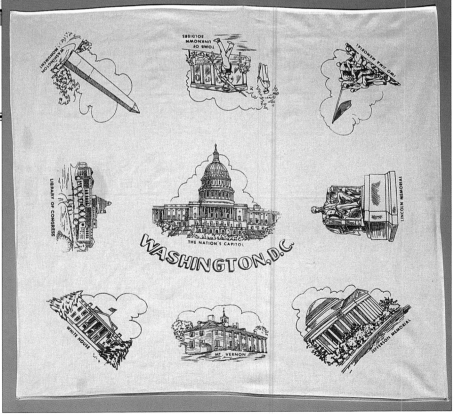

Beautiful 1950s Washington D.C. souvenir tablecloth. This souvenir showcases the famous cherry trees, a gift from Japan in 1912, which signal the coming of spring with an explosion of life and color. 65" x 50". $125-$150.

Wisconsin

Wyoming

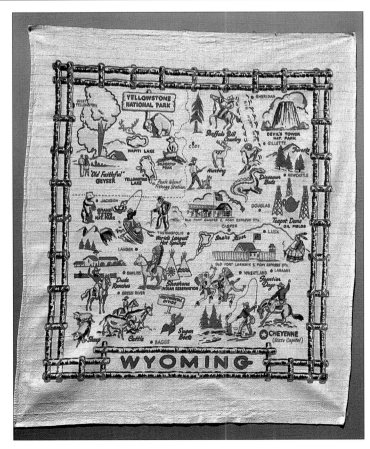

Wisconsin souvenir tablecloth. Over printed design highlighting the state's industries and tourist destinations. 40" x 39". $50-$75. *From the collection of Laura M. Schraeger.*

1930s Wyoming souvenir tablecloth. Interesting political reference to "Teapot Dome," which was the popular name for a scandal during the administration of President Harding. The scandal, which involved the secret leasing of naval oil reserve lands to private companies, was first revealed to the general public in 1924. One cabinet member eventually went to prison for his part in the affair, and a number of Washington officials were implicated. 40" x 40". $150-$175.

Early 1940s Yellowstone National Park tablecloth. Over printed graphics. 38" x 30". $100-$150. *From the collection of Jenny Kuller*.

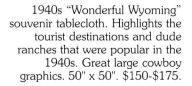

1960s Yellowstone National Park towel. Great graphics of the park wildlife. $20-$25.

1940s "Wonderful Wyoming" souvenir tablecloth. Highlights the tourist destinations and dude ranches that were popular in the 1940s. Great large cowboy graphics. 50" x 50". $150-$175.

Yellowstone Park "In Fact and Fancy" tablecloth. Highlights all the wonderful sites in Yellowstone Park and gives fun, little known facts and trivia. 40" x 40". $100-$150.

1950s Yellowstone Park tablecloth. Bold over printed designs and graphics. 49" x 47". $150-$175.

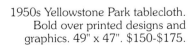

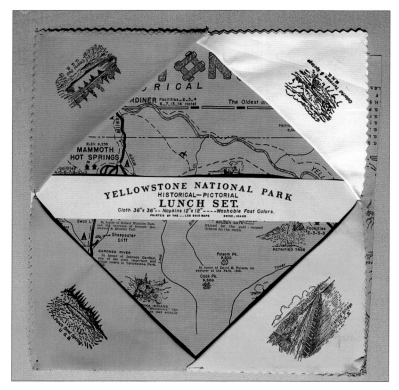

Rare Yellowstone park luncheon set. Realistic one color map of the park that could be used for navigating through the park and then taken home as a souvenir. Manufactured by Paul T. Burdidge, who was famous for his road maps. Copyrighted and dated 1953. 40" x 40". $200-$250.

Detail of the realistic map.

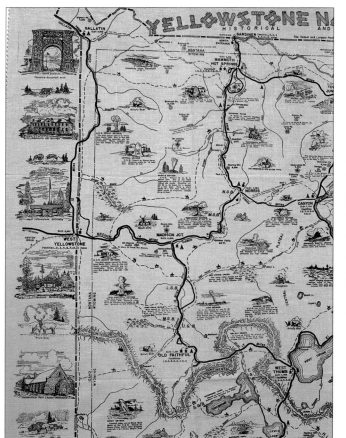

Close-up of the graphics.

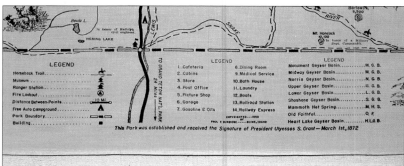

The legend gave additional, much-needed information to the traveler, like the location of rest rooms and hiking trails.

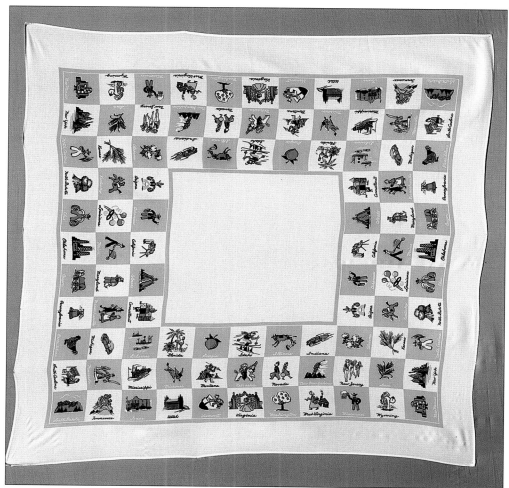

"48 States" tablecloth. During the war, there was an increase in the number of patriotic themed textiles. This one represents the 48 states and was produced by Woodstock Colorama Handprints. They called it "STATEORAMA." It came in several different color combinations and a few years later the company produced the same print again, but with the addition of Alaska, Hawaii, and some of the U.S. territories like "Puerto Rico" and "Wake." 50" x 49". $200-$250. *From the collection of Laura M. Schraeger.*

Close-up of the state graphics.

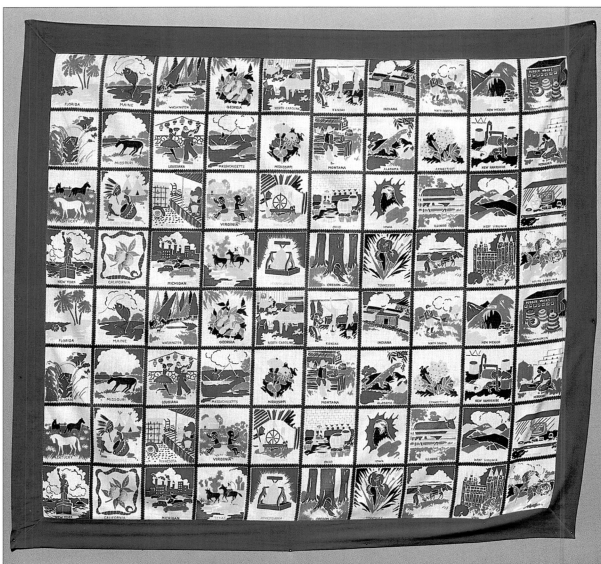

1930s feedsack "States" tablecloth. Large plain cotton "feed and grain bags" used to package many types of dry seeds and grains were a big business in the early part of the twentieth century. With the diverse array of U.S. fabrics and dyes now available, the American colored printed textile sack was born. The thrifty farm community recycled the used sacking and even the string used to sew the bags into table linens and other domestic textile uses. 32" x 30". $125-$150.

Close-up of the state graphics. Note the Black Americana graphic for Virginia.

1946 United States "American Wonderland" tablecloth. Patriotic themed United States map. 1946. Makes reference to Boulder Dam, which changed its name to Hoover Dam in 1947. 50" x 49". $250-$300.

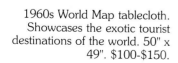

1960s World Map tablecloth. Showcases the exotic tourist destinations of the world. 50" x 49". $100-$150.

Chapter 3

Regional Souvenir Linens

Regional, multi-state linens were also popular as collectibles, as families made cross-country treks through several states during their vacations. Many of the multi-state tablecloths use the graphics of several states to fill in the pattern, creating a more square design. Texas and Oklahoma plus Washington and Oregon are some of the states that you'll find together on one souvenir tablecloth.

Louisiana Purchase

1953 "Louisiana Purchase" tablecloth, produced by Startex. Commemorative 150th anniversary souvenir. This rare tablecloth represents the states purchased under the "Louisiana Purchase" agreement with France in 1803. The Louisiana Purchase stands as the largest area of territory ever added to the U.S. at one time. 50" x 50". $200-$250. *From the collection of Laura M. Schraeger.*

Details of the wonderful corner graphics.

1940s New England regional state tablecloth. Great graphics of the New England region, including a small reference to the "Boston Braves," a baseball team that moved from Boston in 1952. 50" x 49". $150-$175.

Close-up of the wonderful graphics.

1950s New England towel. $40-$50.

Wonderful 1950s New England souvenir scarf. Great graphics. These scarves look terrific draped over side tables. 35" x 36" $40-$60.

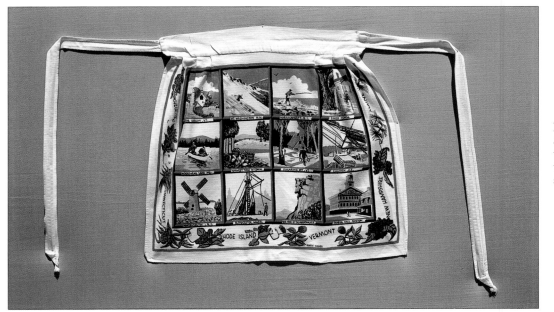

New England souvenir apron. Great representational graphics from the New England states. $30-$45.

Pacific Northwest

1930s Pacific Northwest souvenir tablecloth. Red and blue over printed graphics of the region's industries and tourist destinations. 39" x 40". $100-$150.

Western States

1940s Texas and Oklahoma souvenir tablecloth. Interesting use of colors and very complex designs. 49" x 48". $150-$175.

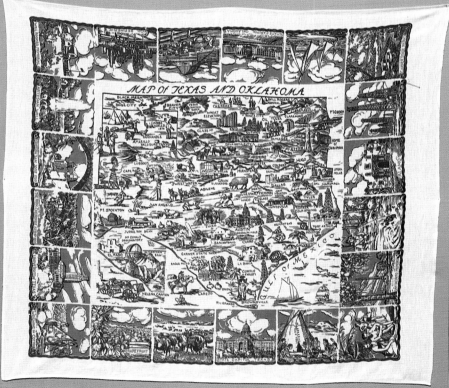

1950s Minnesota, Wisconsin, Michigan souvenir tablecloth. 46" x 44". $150-$175.

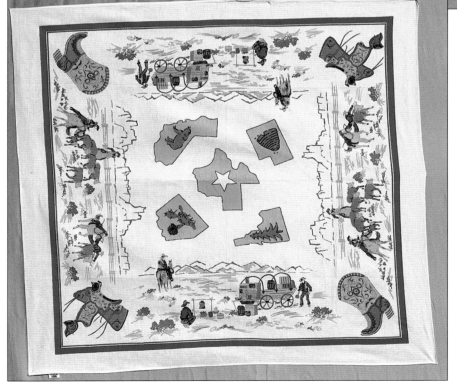

Close-up of the Startex tag.

Western round-up states tablecloth. Produced by Startex in the mid 1950s. Depicts the states that were famous for "cattle drives." 52" x 50". $200-$250.

Bold 1950s western states souvenir scarf. Wonderful graphics and colors of the western half of the United States. 32" x 30". $55-$75.

Chapter 4
World's Fairs and Expositions

1893 Colombian Exposition

The World's Colombian Exposition, celebrating the 400th anniversary of Christopher Columbus's landing in America, was actually held in 1893, a year later than had been planned. New York City, Washington, D.C., St. Louis, and Chicago had all vied for the honor of housing the exposition. President Benjamin Harrison signed the act that designated Chicago as the site of the exposition. It took three frantic years of preparation and work to produce the exposition. Although dedication ceremonies were held on October 21, 1892, the fairgrounds were not opened to the public until May 1, 1893. The exposition closed on October 30, 1893. Most of the souvenir textiles produced for the exposition were turkey red damask show towels with an imprint of Christopher Columbus woven in the center.

1939 New York World's Fair

In April of 1939, the New York World's Fair, "Building The World of Tomorrow," opened on what was once a marshy wasteland in Flushing Meadows, just east of the great metropolis. From its inception to its closing ceremonies, the Fair promoted the belief in science and technology as a means to economic prosperity and personal freedom. Wedged between the greatest economic disaster in America and the growing international tension that would result in World War II, The World of Tomorrow was a much-needed antidote to the depression and confusion of the times. It provided the one saving grace that all of America needed—it provided hope.

1893 World's Fair damask towel. Turkey Red woven edge with George Washington, federal eagles, and cannons jacquard damask design. $150-$175.

1939 mint New York World's Fair tablecloth. Produced by "Bestmaid," with bold deco inspired graphics and details. 39" x 39". $300-$350.

Close-up of the wonderful graphics.

Original Bestmaid label and washing instructions. Both guarantee "Fast Colors." Most Bestmaid cloths will bleed the dye and are NOT colorfastmaking them difficult to find in good condition.

134   *World's Fairs and Expositions*

Within two summers it ran its course, closing in 1940. Several types of souvenir linens are available from this event, including a United States "state" tablecloth designed by Tom Lamb that coordinated with the "Pageant of the States" exhibition and souvenir book. Both the souvenir book and the tablecloth have the same bold deco inspired graphics by Tom Lamb, but the book doesn't credit him for the designs that filled the pages.

1939 New York World's Fair hanky. $45-$75

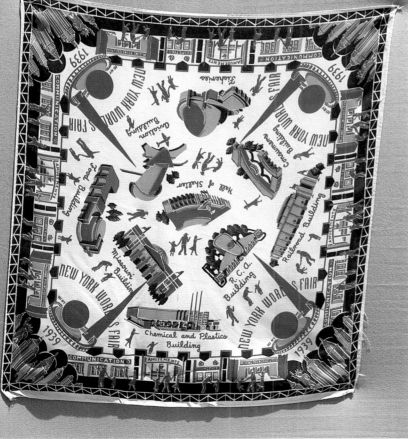

1939 New York World's Fair scarf. Great detail around the edge. 29" x 25". $100-$150.

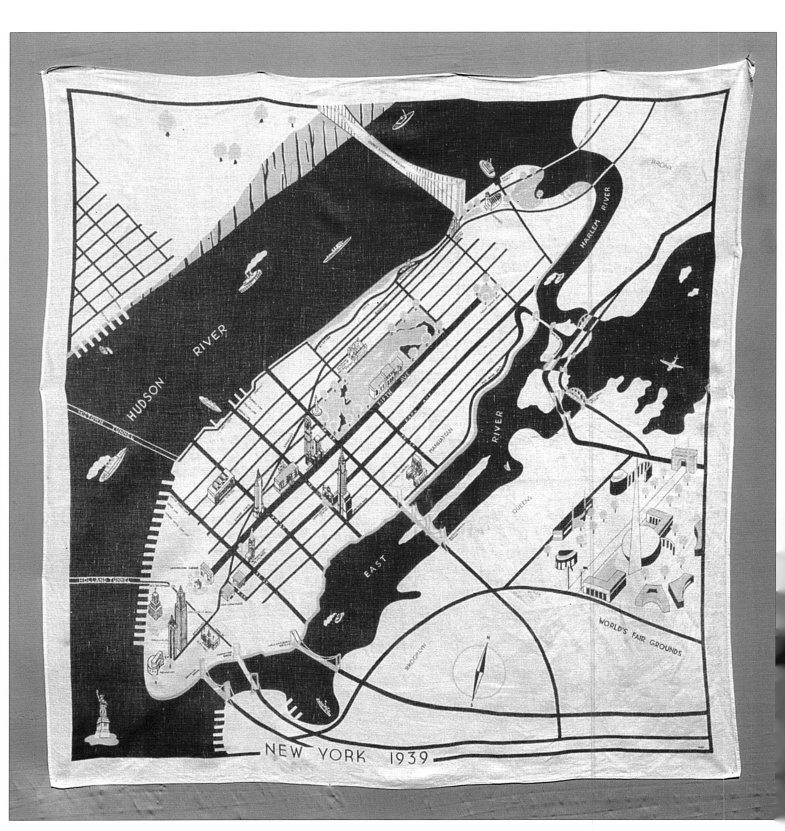

1939 New York tablecloth. Interesting linen tablecloth that shows the
World's Fair location and New York City. 50" x 47". $350-$400.

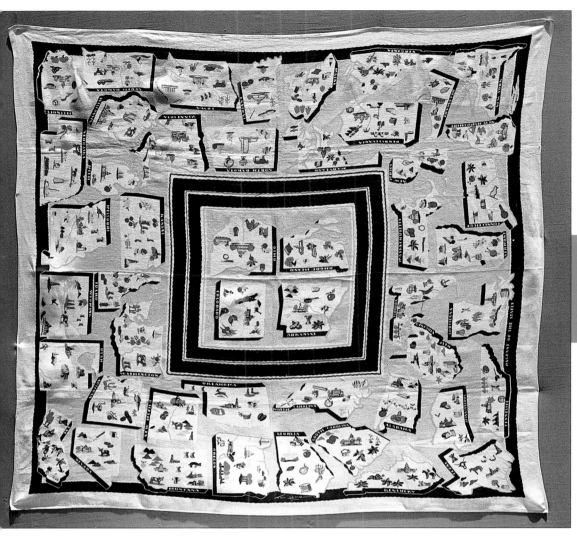

Rare 1939 New York World's Fair "Pageant of the States" tablecloth. Designed by Tom Lamb, this tablecloth was produced to coordinate with a fair exhibit and the book *Pageant of The States* by Dr. Ernest Sutherland Bates & Sr. Herman S. Schiff, published by Random House of New York. The book presented the states one by one with a brief history and acknowledgment of their more illustrious citizens. The illustrations in the book match the tablecloth exactly, with colorful maps showing agricultural and mining products. Small pictures depict noted landmarks and natural attractions. Signed by Tom Lamb. 60" x 50". $400-$575.

Signature of Tom Lamb, a US inventor, industrial designer, and cartoonist, born in New York City in 1897. He studied at the Art Students League and New York University while working for a textile studio. In the 1920s, Mr. Lamb wrote and illustrated children's books and had a monthly page in *Good Housekeeping* magazine called "Kiddyland Movies," which spawned a line of children's products and kitchen textiles.

Pageant of The States by Dr. Ernest Sutherland Bates & Sr. Herman S. Schiff, published by Random House of New York. $50-$65.

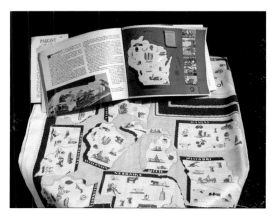

Details of the book and the World's Fair tablecloth. Note that the same graphics for the states that appear in the book are on the tablecloth.

1939 San Francisco
International Exposition

Close-up of the original label.

In 1939, the city of San Francisco hosted an international exhibition, named the Golden Gate Fair in honor of the construction by the city of the world's two largest suspension bridges: the Golden Gate and San Francisco-Oakland, which spanned the San Francisco Bay. With all the skill that could be mustered by American engineers, an island was constructed for the event amidst the pacific waters, becoming the largest ever man made island. Christened Treasure Island, this would be the location of the 1939 Exhibition. The visions of a fair surrounded by the glory of the Pacific Ocean had finally materialized. However, this captivating scene took place as Europe verged on the edge of disaster. Germany had already begun its annexation of neighboring countries and threatened to unleash conflict on a global level.

In only two short years, the United States would be fully involved in this catastrophe. Furthermore, at the time of the fair the United States had just emerged from the Great Depression, which had affected the country in many ways.

1939 International Golden Gate Exposition tablecloth. Mint with the original label. Bright colors opposite the color wheel make a bold statement. 39" x 38". $300-$350.

This fair seemed to provide a brief interlude between these two very difficult times in American history. Many tablecloths and handkerchiefs were produced to commemorate this event, all with bold colors and deco inspired designs.

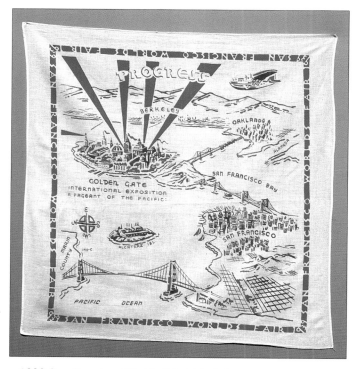

1939 San Francisco Worlds Fair tablecloth. 28" x 25". $50-$75.

1939 Pageant of the Pacific tablecloth. This one has all the titles of the event around the edges. Nice map detail in the center. 39" x 38" $250-$275.

Detail of the deco graphics.

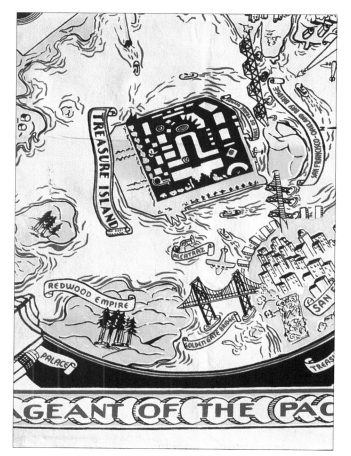

1964 New York World's Fair

The 1964/65 New York World's Fair had two themes that celebrated the future scientific and technological advancements: "Man's Achievements in an Expanding Universe" and "A Millennium of Progress." The fair came at a time when America was at the crest of major scientific and technological advancements that would eventually send a man to the moon and see the harvesting of nuclear power and the development of computer technology for the betterment of mankind.

The exhibits showcased the two themes with atomic and space graphics and bold surreal architecture. The souvenir textiles from this fair are boldly colored, with atomic space graphics. Most are over printed with gold or silver metallic dyes.

1964 New York World's Fair apron. $50-$75.

Chapter 5

Dating Souvenir Linens

Overview

As the tourist industry in each state changed, so did the souvenir linen, and sometimes we can use these changes to generally determine dates. Dude ranches, auto camps, and small tourist venues came and went as the tourist landscape changed. Dating the souvenir linen you have solely by the graphics is not recommended, as designers used older model cars and the same graphic designs of people for twenty years or more. However, most of the time the tourist attractions were updated regularly, so a quick check on the history of a specific tourist destination is a more accurate way to date your souvenir.

It is relatively easy to date souvenir tablecloths by researching the tourist attractions shown, and sometimes the general date can be determined based on which landmarks are pictured on the cloth. For example, in California, "Boulder Dam" changed its name to "Hoover Dam" in 1947, and Disneyland opened in 1955. In Florida, Walt Disney World didn't open until 1971. The Utah state tablecloth shown can be dated to the early 1930s by looking at the National Parks. Dinosaur National Monument was established in 1932, and Zion and Bryce National Parks (misspelled on this tablecloth as "Brice") were established prior to 1932. This tablecloth highlights some attractions that were only popular in the late 1920s and early 1930s. Peach produce farms were a thriving industry in Utah until the late 1930s. This is a great example of an early one-color state souvenir tablecloth.

Dating a souvenir using the graphics on the cloth can be misleading. This 1920s auto camp with vintage cars can be found on a 1970s Florida souvenir tablecloth.

Although in some cases tablecloths can be assigned to a general decade as in this book or even to a specific group of years, the lack of manufacturing records or other cataloguing of these delightful keepsakes makes assigning any one date extremely difficult. For example, many tablecloth patterns were produced during a specific year, and if they remained popular, they were available to the consumer for many years after their original date of production. There are, however, many useful clues to assist in the dating of tablecloths, which can be found through a study of period fabrics, designs, colors, and styles.

Just as fashions changed and evolved thorough the decades, so did styles of the vintage tablecloth. Certain patterns and fabrics enjoyed popularity during specific years. For example, 100% linen tablecloths were fashionable up until the late 1930s, then cotton rayon blends were introduced and enjoyed popularity for their easy care properties.

Vintage 1940s tablecloth graphic that makes fun of the "Hoover Dam" name changes. It was originally named "Hoover Dam" in 1930, then "Boulder Dam" from 1931-1945, then back to "Hoover Dam" in 1946.

During this same period, Yucca Prints and Cactus Prints manufactured their tablecloths using a thick burlap material, which they called "cactus cloth." After the 1940s you will find the same designs of tablecloths offered in many different choices of fabrics, like cotton, linen, and rayon blends, as well as in many color variations. They will also be found with matching napkins and in a larger size for the family dinner table.

The following information on the types of printing processes will assist you in dating your linens. Many tablecloths show evidence of missing or significantly faded colors referred to as "fugitive dyes," since true "color-fast" dyes were not created until the early 1940s. Most tablecloths with signs of fugitive dyes indicate a pre-1935 date, although you will also find fugitive dyes appearing in tablecloths that were produced during World War II when good quality dyes were scarce. Over dyed and over printed patterns, along with a count of the number of colors used in the pattern, can also help you determine the approximate age of your tablecloth. If the tablecloth contains a tag or paper label, there is a wealth of information at your fingertips and you will be better able to identify the period of manufacture. Government regulations changed the information required on these tags, and certain dated terms were used to give the consumer greater confidence in the tablecloth, such as "Fast Colors" and "Sanforized." At the end of this chapter there is a brief summary of the clues you may use to date your tablecloth for quick reference.

Types of Printing Processes

Fabrics with colored designs are known as printed cloths. The printing of cloth represents an important part of the tablecloth manufacturing process. Early printed tablecloths were hand stamped simple designs, usually of a single color. Most of these early souvenirs were pillow covers or small tea cloths from national parks. As the printing process improved, more colors and increasingly elaborate designs were possible, allowing tablecloth designers to create more intricate and detailed designs. Identifying the printing process used on your tablecloth can be difficult, but if accomplished, this can be another useful tool for dating your tablecloth collection. Manufacturers used a variety of methods for printing fabrics. These are explained below.

Hand Blocking

Before the method of direct roller printing was discovered, textiles were printed by hand. Hand blocking gave a greater variety of designs and color effects, as the regular repetition of a pattern that is necessary in the roller method is not necessary in hand blocking. A block of wood, copper, or other material bearing a design in relief with the dye paste applied to the surface is pressed on the fabric. Linen was the fabric of choice for hand blocking because it has the proper texture and quality. One

way to detect hand blocking is to look along the selvage for the regularity of the repetition of the design. In roller printing, the design must be repeated at regular intervals. With hand blocking, one color runs into another in at least a few places, and the design may be uneven due to the "block" unevenly stamping the design across the tablecloth. You can find this type of printing on one color, smaller souvenirs from the 1920s.

Direct or Copper Roller Printing

Developed in 1810, this is the simplest method of printing tablecloths and probably the most used up until the mid 1940s. The fabric was carried on a rotating central cylinder and pressed by a series of rollers, each bearing one color. Large bolts of fabric were stitched together to assure a continuous print of the design on the tablecloth. The design was engraved on the copper rollers by hand or machine pressure or etched by photoengraving methods. The color paste was applied to the rollers through feed rollers rotating in a color box. Earlier tablecloths were simple two color designs but by the late 1930s, as many as eight colors could be printed very quickly. Sometimes you can find a tablecloth that was printed over the binding stitching between bolts of cloth. These cloths were usually given away to the employees for use in their homes and can occasionally be found today on on-line auction sites. They are a quirky, fun example of the early printing processes used for these vintage linens.

This California souvenir tablecloth shows how two bolts of fabric were quickly stitched together to make a continuous run. Sometimes the design was printed over the stitching.

Resist Printing

In this method, the design is printed first with a chemical paste. The paste is so concentrated that when the cloth is dyed, the parts covered with the paste don't take the dye, leaving the design in the original cloth color. This can be seen in the late 1930s California highway souvenir tablecloth.

Example of a resist printed cloth.

Over Dying

A method in which one color is placed over another to create a third color or to add to the design is called over dying or over printing. It is usually done as a screen printing process. An example of this would be blue over printed with yellow to make green, or red over printed with blue to make purple. You can find many tablecloths today that demonstrate evidence of this printing style. It shows up almost as if it were a case of sloppy printing. The colors lay over one another, crowding the design or resulting in a design that is not evenly aligned. These tablecloths were most likely produced from the late 1920s to the early 1940s.

Example of an over dyed cloth. Yellow and blue dyes were printed over each other to make a green.

Screen Printing

This is a method of printing somewhat like stenciling. It is accomplished by using a screen, generally made of fine mesh cloth. The areas of the screen through which the coloring passed were filled with waterproof varnish or other insoluble filler. The color, in the form of a paste, was then forced through the untreated portions of the screen onto the fabric underneath. During World War I, screen-printing took off as an industrial printing process. This process was what tablecloth manufacturers were referring to when they used the term "Hand Printed." It was mainly used at first for flags and banners but was quickly adopted for printing tablecloths from the 1920s up until approximately 1948.

Example of an automated screen printed cloth with more complex design and colors.

Over Printing

Early 1930s and 1940s tablecloths were hand screened and usually employed over printing to create the patterns. The printer first layered a single color design across the fabric then, using another design screen, laid the second color and pattern across the fabric. This was repeated until the design was completed. Most over printed cloth designs will be slightly off, since each one was hand screened and each layer was applied individually.

Grinning

An interesting technique found in screen printed cloths is "grinning." Grinning is the use of halos of white to separate graphics and multiple colors. This technique enabled textile printers to produce yards of fabric more quickly with less chance of an accidental overlap of colors. You can find many tablecloths where this printing technique is evident, and it is a good way to date your tablecloths. This technique is usually found in the earlier souvenir linens produced between 1930 and 1940.

Automated Screen Printing Machine

This process was thought to have been first installed by the Printex Company in California for their Vera Tablecloth line in 1946. This method advanced and automated the screen printing process, speeding up the method and allowing more creativity and flexibility for the tablecloth designer. You can identify automated screen printed tablecloths by looking for color variations in the shading. They also show a more detailed and crisper design. These tablecloths are beautiful, with complex colors and designs giving them a more three dimensional look. Most of these types of tablecloths were produced after 1948 and are usually much bigger cloths.

Example of an over printed cloth. Each color graphic was printed separately, so the design sometimes "misses" and looks slightly off.

Example of a grinning, with wide areas of white surrounding the lettering and some of the graphics. An indication of an early 1930s-1940s printing style.

Quick
Reference Summary

Victorian: 1840-1899
- Turkey Red damasks
- Dark crimsons, maroons, browns, gold colors
- Velvets
- Felted table covers

Art Nouveau: 1900
- Deep wine color
- Turkey Red damasks
- Crisp linen damasks
- Browns
- Dark cheddar yellow
- Green, purple were fugitive dyes

World War I: 1910s
- Pastel colors
- One directional designs
- Stamped designs, one color on linen
- Turkey Red damasks without fringe

Art Deco: 1920s
- More use of pastel colors
- No "true" greens, but light sage was possible
- Pastel colors in opposites of the color wheel
- Lighter color red
- Increase in number of printed colors (two or more)
- Designs are larger and usually in the corners

The Depression: 1930s
- Bright, clear, multi-color prints up to three colors
- Colors opposite the color wheel, i.e., orange/blue, orange/green, purple/yellow
- Large areas of grinning/shadowing around motifs
- Increase in "imports" from Japan, Czechoslovakia, Ireland
- "Vat Dyed," "Merchanized," "Made in the USA" terms used

World War II: 1940s
- Use of terms "hand printed," "Made in America," "Color Fast," "Sanforized"
- Locations of military installations and/or reference to military vehicles, planes or ships
- "OPA" Office of Price Administration price sticker (1942-1947)
- Use of the term "Screen printed"
- Four+ color combinations
- 1946: Delicate shading in designs; more "realistic" three dimensional designs
- State souvenir tablecloths in larger sizes with coordinating napkins
- Rayon/Cotton "blends"

Prosperity: 1950s
- Continuation of 1940s designs but with richer colors and patterns
- More use of bold synthetic dyes
- Metallic dyes, especially gold and silver
- Metallic threads running throughout
- Synthetic fabrics
- Rayon
- Polyester
- Black outlined designs
- 1958: Percentage of fibers in fabrics labeled, e.g., 20% rayon 80% Cotton
- Designer "signed" souvenir linens

Reproductions and New "Vintage Style" Souvenirs

There are a number of vintage tablecloth reproductions on the market today, which can be confusing for the general tablecloth collector. Most reproductions I have found either still retain the new manufacturer's tag by Moda, or have been represented as "reproduction" or "vintage look" tablecloths by the dealers. There are, however, a few people that have either knowingly or unknowingly misrepresented a reproduction tablecloth as vintage. I have found several people on on-line auction sites representing a reproduction "Texas" state map tablecloth and "Vacationland" United States map tablecloth as vintage and selling them for up to $80. They can be purchased at most on-line web stores for $40-$50.

Here are a few tips to keep in mind when purchasing a "vintage" tablecloth. Most vintage linens collected today were produced anywhere from 25 to 125 years ago and will show signs of age. Even a "mint with tag" tablecloth will have slight yellowing in the fold lines or areas of discoloration. Spending a few minutes to educate yourself can save you many dollars in the future on misrepresented reproduction tablecloths.

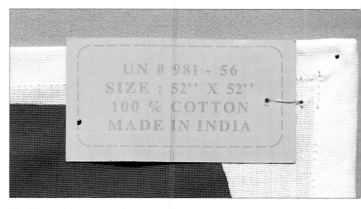

Moda tag. Most reproductions on the market today are manufactured by "Moda" and should have a sewn in label, unless it has been removed.

Vintage Tablecloths	Reproduction Tablecloths
Will have signs of age, discoloration	Will be crisp, new
Made from a variety of quality fabrics	Made from low grade fabrics
Made with rich, colorful dyes	Made with flat or dull colors
Have two small hems hemmed with wide hems	Have all four sides

Reproduction souvenir tablecloths can be a fun way of adding that vintage look to your dining room and are sometimes easier on your wallet than the fifty-year-old originals. Since they are found in large quantities, you can have entire rooms filled with reproduction tablecloths for luncheons, parties, or even weddings. You can also rest assured that if one of these becomes stained or damaged, another can be purchased to replace it. Several sources where you can purchase these fun reproduction linens are listed in the resource section at the back of this book.

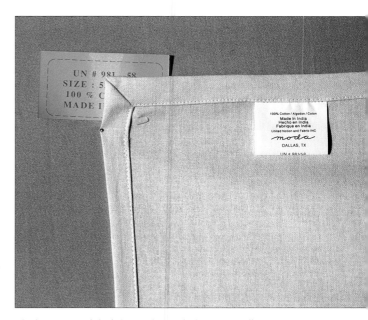

Moda sewn in label. Note the wide hems on all four sides, an indication of a Moda cloth.

Florida reproduction
towel. Thin cotton. $5-$7.

California reproduction towel. $5-$7.

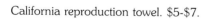

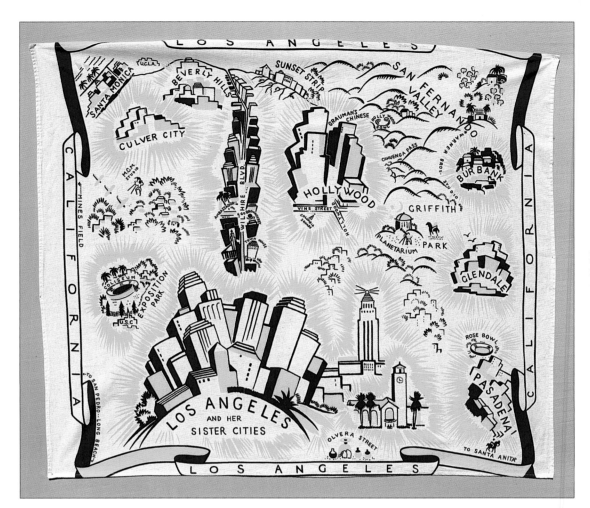

Los Angeles reproduction fabric made into a tablecloth. $10-$20.

Florida souvenir towel. Nice thick woven cotton. Unknown maker. $10-$15.

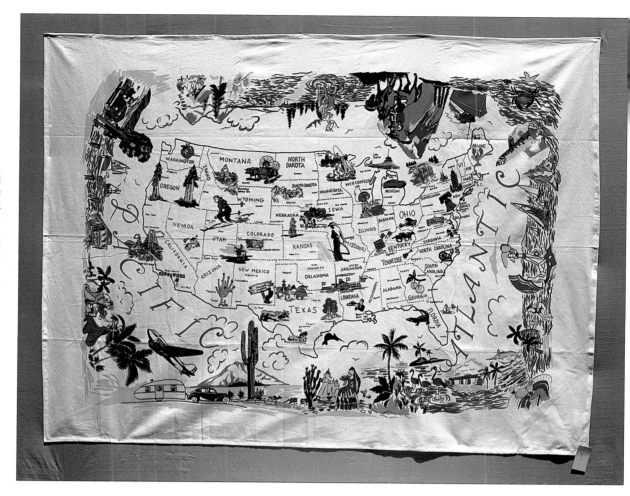

Moda "United States" vintage style tablecloth. Thick cotton, 68" x 50". This shrinks considerably when washed so you'll find it in smaller sizes as well. $35-$50.

Moda "Vacationland" vintage style tablecloth. 70" x 50". Again, this shrinks, so watch the size.

Moda "East Coast" vintage style tablecloth. The graphics were
taken from a vintage New Jersey tablecloth. $40-$55.

Chapter 7

Stain Removal Guide

My best advice for a vintage souvenir linen collector is not to be deterred from purchasing tablecloths with stains or small pinholes. Most yellow stains can be almost completely removed or lightened significantly by following a few simple guidelines. I enjoy displaying tablecloths with a few small holes and even those with slight stains. I believe they add character and charm to a wonderfully loved piece with a rich history. These slight imperfections are the result of years of Sunday dinners, family celebrations, and intimate dinner parties. People loved, laughed, and cried over these precious tablecloths, and I'm proud to own them.

These wonderful tablecloths are anywhere from 50 to 125+ years old and were used and cherished, so they will naturally show signs of use. My perfect linens are carefully stored and only brought out for "show," but my used, treasured ones with slight holes and imperfections, are brought out daily and lovingly used with no fear of further damaging them. In fact, we add to their charm with our own little stains and rips. These "imperfect" tablecloths warm our kitchen and brighten our lives. My family is happy to cherish and use each one, knowing that each stain and imperfection is a part of its long history.

The same tablecloth, "after." Following some of the guidelines in this chapter, most of the stains have been removed or lightened significantly.

A vintage 1930s Florida souvenir tablecloth and napkins, "before." Surface dirt and storage stains.

General Guidelines

First check your tablecloth to determine its approximate age (see Chapter 5: Dating Souvenir Linens). Tablecloths made prior to 1935 will have dyes that may not be colorfast and may fade or clean unevenly. Watch for any signs of the colors running out of the cloth. The water will be tinged with red, green, or orange. Remove the tablecloth immediately and rinse in cold water.

Always check your tablecloth while you are soaking or cleaning it to watch for fading colors or possible disintegration of the fabric. Here's a tip from Martha Stewart: Line your wash basin with a sheet before filling it with soap. Place larger or more fragile pieces in the basin to soak. When you are through, simply lift the material by the corners to remove from the basin. This will help keep fragile fabrics and linens from stretching or other damage.

Do not knead, twist, or push the tablecloth too hard when removing the excess water from the cloth. This will further damage and rip any areas where the fabric is thin.

Make sure the tablecloth is free from significant wear holes that may be made larger by vigorous washing.

I have found that nature is the best bleacher. Hanging tablecloths from a clothesline or laying them outside on a sheet in the grass after washing will do a beautiful job of lightening yellow stains. Make sure that if you hang your tablecloth on the clothesline, you are not stretching the ends. Use several clothespins to hang it straight across the line.

Definitions

Detergent: All-purpose synthetic detergent (liquid or powder). Use liquid detergent full strength. Mix powder with water to form a paste when working into stain.

Powdered, non-chlorine bleach: Powdered, bleach product such as "Biz" may be used to remove stains by soaking fabric in tepid water for length of time.

Dry-cleaning solvents: Stain and spot removers available at grocery and hardware stores. A nonflammable type is safest to use.

Stain Stick: An enzyme-based cleaner available at grocery and discount stores. Most effective on food, grease, oil, protein, and dirt-based stains and can be used on any fabric and color. Can remain on fabric for up to one week.

Out Darn Spot!

If you know what type of stain is on the cloth, the following suggestions are very helpful for removing new and sometimes older stains.

Alcoholic Drinks, Wine

Launder with detergent in the hottest water safe for the fabric. If it is a new stain, do not use soap (bar, flake, or detergents containing natural soap), since soap could make the stain permanent or at least much more difficult to remove.

For old stains, soak in a solution of water with one half of a scoop of powdered non-chlorine bleach. Watch carefully. Soak for at least two hours (more if necessary). Line dry in sun.

Soak tough stains for thirty minutes in one quart of warm water and one teaspoon of enzyme presoak product.

The removal of old or set-in stains may require washing with non-chlorine powdered bleach that is safe for the fabric. Always check for colorfastness first.

If all the sugars from the wine or alcohol are not removed, a brown stain will appear when the fabric is heated in the dryer or is ironed, as the sugar becomes caramelized in the heat.

Blood

Treat new blood stains immediately!

Flush cold water through the stain and scrape off crusted material.

Soak for fifteen minutes in a mixture of one quart lukewarm water, one half teaspoon liquid hand dishwashing detergent, and one tablespoon ammonia. Use cool/lukewarm water.

Rub gently from the back to loosen stain.

Soak for another fifteen minutes in above mixture. Rinse. Soak in an enzyme product for at least thirty minutes. Soak aged stains for several hours. Launder normally.

If the blood stain is not completely removed by this process, wet the stain with hydrogen peroxide and a few drops of ammonia. Caution: Do not leave this mixture on the cloth longer than fifteen minutes. Rinse with cool water.

If the blood stain has dried, pre-treat the area with pre-wash stain remover, liquid laundry detergent, or a paste of granular laundry product and water. Launder using bleach that is safe for the type of fabric.

Candle Wax

Harden the wax by rubbing with ice. Remove the surface wax by carefully scraping with the dull edge of a butter knife. If that does not work, you can try the next suggestion.

Sandwich the wax stain between folded paper towels and press down lightly on top of the towel with a warm (not hot) iron. Replace the paper towels frequently to absorb more wax and to prevent transferring the stain to new areas. Continue as long as wax is being removed.

Coffee, Tea

Saturate the stain with a pretreatment stain remover.

Rub the stain with a heavy-duty liquid detergent and launder in the hottest water safe for the fabric.

If it is a new stain, do not use soap (bar, flake, or detergents containing natural soap), since soap could make the stain permanent or at least more difficult to remove.

For old stains, soak the tablecloth in a solution of water with one half scoop powdered non-chlorine bleach. Watch carefully. Soak for at least two hours (more if necessary). Line dry in sun.

Dye Stains/Dye Transfer

Soak the entire tablecloth in a diluted solution of powdered non-chlorine bleach.

If the stain remains and the tablecloth is colorfast, soak the entire tablecloth in a dilute solution of liquid chlorine bleach and water. Always test for colorfastness first (see below) and watch carefully. Caution: Chlorine bleach may change the color of the tablecloth or cause irreversible damage, especially in pre-1930s tablecloths. If the stain does not come out within fifteen minutes of bleaching, it cannot be removed by this method and any further exposure to bleach will weaken the fabric and remove the color. I do not recommend this for general stain removal or for tablecloths that were made prior to 1935. Check the dating information in Chapter 5 for clues regarding the tablecloths' approximate age.

Note: To check for colorfastness to liquid chlorine bleach, mix one tablespoon of bleach with one quarter cup of water. Use an eyedropper to put a drop of this solution on a hidden seam in the tablecloth. Let stand two minutes, then blot dry. If there is no color change, it is probably safe to use the product. Powdered non-chorine bleaches have directions for colorfastness tests on their boxes.

There are also a number of dye removers/strippers that are available in drug and grocery stores. Be careful, however, as color removers will take out fabric colors as well as the stain.

Mildew

Mildew is a growing organism that must have warmth, darkness, and moisture to survive. Mildew actually eats cotton and linen fibers and can also attack manufactured fibers, causing permanent damage and a weakening of fibers and fabrics. It is very difficult to remove and will damage the value of a vintage tablecloth.

To treat mildew, first carefully brush or shake off the mildewed area. Pre-treat the stains by rubbing the areas with a heavy-duty liquid detergent. Then launder in the hottest water safe for the fabric, using bleach safe for fabric. Always check for colorfastness and for the age of the tablecloth before using any type of bleach. Let the item dry in the sun.

Badly mildewed fabric may be damaged beyond repair. Old stains may respond to flushing with dry cleaning fluids. Carefully read and follow the instructions on the product label.

Rust

Removing rust stains can be difficult; these stains cannot be removed with normal laundering. Do not use chlorine bleach, as chlorine bleach will make the stains permanent.

Small stains may be removed with a few drops of a commercial rust remover or by repeated applications of lemon juice and salt on the stain. Do not let the fabric dry between applications.

Rinse thoroughly and launder with a liquid laundry detergent and oxygen color safe bleach or powdered non-chlorine bleach. If safe for the specific fabric try this old home remedy: first, boil fabric in a solution of four teaspoons of cream of tartar per pint of water. Rinse thoroughly.

Rust removers that contain hydrofluoric acid are extremely toxic, can burn the skin, and will damage the porcelain finish on appliances and sinks. Use as a last resort.

Scorch/Burn Marks

Scorching permanently damages the fabric. The heat burns and weakens the fibers and can also melt manufactured fibers, such as polyester. If the damage is slight you may be able to improve the look. Brush the area to remove any charring.

If the tablecloth is washable, rub liquid detergent into the scorched area, then launder.

If the stain remains, bleach with an all-fabric non-chlorine bleach.

Smoke/Odors

Some older tablecloths that have been stored for many years have an "old" smell and yellowing in the creases. You will also find tablecloths that have been in a smoker's home and have that "telltale" smoke odor. I have not had any problems removing either of these odors from my tablecloths.

If the tablecloth is not seriously frayed or damaged in any other way, soak it in a solution of tepid water and one scoop of powdered non-chlorine bleach. Watch carefully for any signs of dyes fading. Remove immediately if you see green or red "tinged" water.

Soak overnight and place outside out all day in the sun. Repeat if necessary, but this should work in one treatment.

Tomato-based Stains

Saturate the area with pretreatment laundry stain remover. Wait a couple of minutes for the product to penetrate the stain. For stubborn stains, rub with heavy-duty liquid detergent. Launder immediately.

If the stain remains, soak the entire tablecloth in a diluted solution of all-fabric powdered bleach. Be aware that all the colors may lighten.

If the stain persists and the tablecloth is white or colorfast, soak in a diluted solution of liquid chlorine bleach and water. However, be sure to read the tablecloth label regarding the use of bleach. Bleach can damage some dyes and prints, and bleaching damage is irreversible. Also,

if the stain is not removed in fifteen minutes, it cannot be removed by bleaching and further bleaching will only weaken the fabric.

Yellowing, Graying

For old stains, soak the tablecloth in a solution of water with one half scoop of powdered non-chlorine bleach. Watch carefully. Look for signs that the dye is colorfast. Soak for at least four hours (more if necessary). Line dry in the sun. Repeat the process if still yellow.

Chapter 8

Care and Storage of Vintage Linens

Displaying Your Treasures

Sunlight is a vintage tablecloth's worst enemy. Exposed for long periods of time in direct sunlight, a tablecloth will fade unevenly. If you are using a tablecloth on a table that is in the sun, make sure you replace the cloth often, at least once a week.

Tablecloths look great rolled and stacked in an old open wooden "ice box" or small glass display cabinet. Draped over a whitewashed old ladder or layered on your dinner table, vintage tablecloths add charm to any home and are guaranteed to bring smiles to the guests at your next dinner party or barbecue.

If you have some of your tablecloths displayed in these ways, you might find this suggestion helpful in "storing" and preserving the rest of your treasures. Instead of folding the tablecloth after it is cleaned and dried, take a paper gift wrap tube and roll the tablecloth around it. Then pin in place and stack upright in a closet. This prevents fold lines, which accumulate dust and dirt and weaken the fibers. If you must fold the tablecloths, take them out occasionally, inspect them, and refold another way. If you are going to store the tablecloths in a drawer, wrap them in acid-free tissue paper (available at specialty paper stores). This will protect them from disintegrating.

In this age of new, modern designs, fast cars, and even faster computers, it is refreshing to pull out a vintage tablecloth and instantly be transported back to a simpler place and time. Surrounded by darling and whimsical souvenir designs, we can all take a moment to appreciate the "good life" of days gone by, and reflect on our own place in this fast paced, hectic world.

Restoring "Mint With Tag" Vintage Linens

I am fortunate enough to have a large selection of "mint with the paper tag" vintage tablecloths. Since these trea-

sures were stored and unused for many years, they show signs of dirt accumulation in the fold lines. Dirt, over a period of time, will weaken the fibers and become more difficult to remove. Paper tags will also become brittle and disintegrate over time.

I wanted to use my mint tablecloths, but also retain the original tags with the tablecloths. To me, the labels are as interesting as the tablecloths themselves. They are a wonderful source of knowledge, have great graphics, and they give useful information about the manufacturers.

In order to preserve these special treasures, I carefully remove the paper label and, if it is extremely fragile, affix it to a piece of acid free cardstock. Then I use a cold small laminator (available at any craft or stationary store) to carefully laminate it with double-sided laminate. After restoring the vintage tablecloth, I attach the laminated tag to the corner of the tablecloth with a small gold safety pin and a pretty ribbon. I can then use the tablecloth or display it, in restored condition, along with its original tag.

Creative Crafts

When a vintage tablecloth has too many holes or cannot be restored for use as a tablecloth, there are still many other ways to enjoy your treasure. There is nothing a dedicated crafter enjoys more than trying to make that last little scrap of material into something useful, decorative, or wearable. Old tablecloths with holes, rips, or faded areas sacrifice themselves willingly to every imaginable type of crafting project. With very little work, even the most damaged tablecloth treasure can become a summer beach outfit, a beautiful party dress, a teddy bear, a quilt, a new lampshade, or a purse. Tablecloths can also be made into covers for picture frames, diaries, photo albums, and even button covers. In fact, there is no end to the creative ideas for using pieces of vintage tablecloths. Here are just a few suggestions for unique presents you can make as gifts or just to indulge yourself. Your imagination and a strong sense of "fun" will help you create your own one-of-a-kind items out of precious old souvenir tablecloths.

Children's Clothing

Souvenir tablecloths make an ideal fabric for children's and even adult clothing. The material is soft and you know the colors will last, since they have already been washed many times. And even if there are a few holes, you can cut around any flaws in the material. There are many clothing and craft patterns available. Simply choose one that suits your sewing experience and begin.

The easiest way to cut out clothing is to first cut out the paper pattern pieces you will actually be using, then iron them with a cool iron so they are not wrinkled. Lay out the tablecloth material on a flat surface and be sure to mark the holes or other flaws in some way.

The front and back pieces of the garment should be cut out first, as you will most likely want to feature the predominant pattern from the tablecloth on these panels and they will also take the largest amounts of fabric. Find the best part of the tablecloth and fold it, keeping the fold where you want the middle of the front piece to be, then cut out the front piece. Even small tablecloths will have enough useable "picture" area to cut a nice design for the front. Either do the same for the back piece or find two similar sections and cut the back section twice. If you want to be really daring, you can even cut out one of the back pieces right side up, and the other one upside down or sideways. There are no absolute rules for assembling this delightful tablecloth "puzzle" that will become your new garment!

Darling little girl's dress and matching purse made from vintage Florida tablecloth.

Girl's dress and matching purse made by taking a polka dot dress and adding details from a vintage Florida tablecloth.

Another little girl's dress made by adding a vintage Florida table-cloth skirt to a pink shirt.

A vintage California tablecloth
with holes and stains finds
new life as a dress and
matching purse.

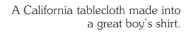

A California tablecloth made into
a great boy's shirt.

Matthew and Michelle enjoying
a day at the beach.

Little boy's shirt made from a vintage Alaska tablecloth with holes and stains.

Miss Audrey and Miss Olivia enjoy their state tablecloth dresses, purses, hats, and matching bears.

Next, cut out the other parts of the garment from the material that remains. If you are making sleeves, you can either try to match the pattern from the front panel or cut out something to contrast with it. Areas like sleeves, pockets, and even collars or facings can also be cut out of material you purchase that matches or contrasts with the tablecloth pattern.

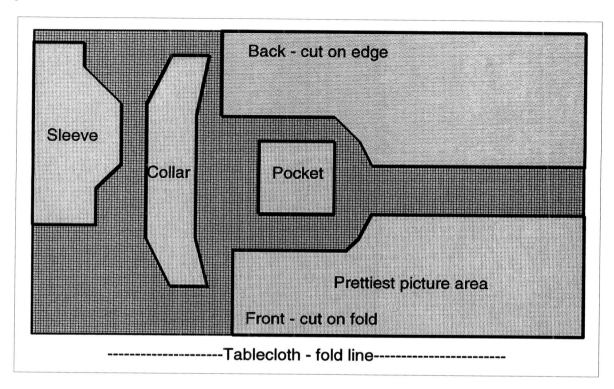

The same techniques can be used for a large purse. Cut a large square out of the most beautiful pattern from the tablecloth, then use the leftover areas for the back side of the purse, the straps, and the lining. Or you can purchase material to line the purse and to make those "secret pockets" that we all love so much.

Always keep the scraps from your project. You can use them to cover buttons for a sudden and surprising decorator detail on an existing sweater, dress, jacket, or child's clothing item, or use the buttons on something new. Even the smallest pieces of brightly colored tablecloth make cute teddy bears, mice, or other animals. And they are easily glued onto frames or used for any other craft items.

Other Fun Ideas

•Give your old lampshade a new look. Make a paper template to fit around the shade. Cut out your tablecloth using the template pattern, leaving a 2" edge at the top and bottom. Hot glue this material to the outside of the lampshade, then fold over the edges and glue to the back of the shade. Be sure to fold over the material on the top and bottom before gluing in place. Easy, fast, and fun.

A simple store-bought straw purse embellished with vintage linens.

• Cover a plain address book or photo album with a piece of vintage linen for instant nostalgia. You could also cover a diary, recipe book, or box to hold recipes.

• Tablecloths make great pillows. Add some vintage chenille and trim and you have a wonderful "cottage chic" pillow.

• Quilters, you already know what to do. Go for it! It would be absolutely wonderful to mix tablecloth fabric with the modern fabrics that are available for quilters today.

• Make a cloth doll or stuffed animal with scraps of different tablecloths. Roosters are a great choice when you want to use up every little bit of that precious souvenir tablecloth. Each feather can be made from a different cloth or scrap of material. Mix in a few solid colors for a truly original creation.

• Cover a small corkboard with a vintage tablecloth. Add some wooden details and cute push pins.

• Redecorate your garden patio with a tablecloth and matching tablecloth pillows. Or use scraps and pieces from all those "cutters" to create groupings of colorful pillows for your lawn furniture and patio.

• Make a picture frame. Wrap and secure with tacks and glue small remnants of tablecloths around a wooden frame. Add a bow or some decorative buttons for charm. These make great presents, especially if the frame features old graphics and pictures from a home state or favorite vacation spot.

• Make a romantic, cottage chic wooden serving tray. Find a wooden tray at a yard sale or buy one at a craft store. Cut a piece of tablecloth to fit the inside of the tray. Using adhesive spray, carefully spray the inside of the tray, then place a piece of vintage tablecloth inside. Have a small piece of glass cut for the inside of the tray. Finish with a few small nails to hold the glass in place.

Two handbags made fabulous with vintage souvenir linens.

• Find a tablecloth with a simple border and plain white center. Take it to your next reunion or party and have the guests sign it with paint pens. An instant "future souvenir collectible."

Lampshade covered with vintage souvenir tablecloth fabric.

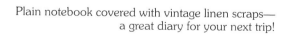

Plain notebook covered with vintage linen scraps—
a great diary for your next trip!

Fun crafts from vintage souvenir linens.

Vintage linens make wonderfully soft stuffed animals using a pattern from your local fabric store.

A sweet 18" bear from a United States reproduction tablecloth.

A quick and easy weekend craft project.

Of all the animals, these are my favorites—darling roosters
made from a combination of vintage and new fabrics.

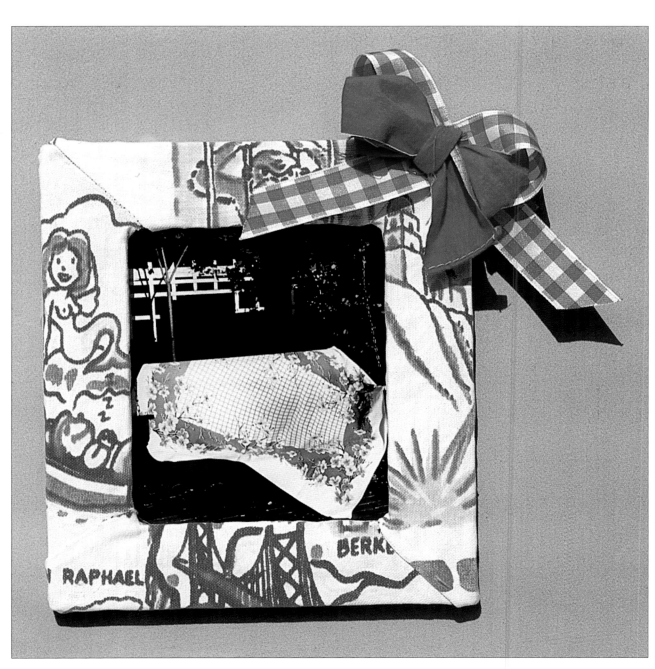

Vintage linen used to cover a plain wooden frame—what
better way to display vacation photos?

Plain wooden serving tray made fabulous with
some paint and a vintage Florida tablecloth.

Chapter 10

Tablecloth
Manufacturers: 1840-1960

Most of these tablecloth manufacturers produced only printed tablecloth designs; a few produced souvenir linens as well. This information can be used to date your tablecloths and to learn more about the history of vintage linens in general.

Abraham & Straus, 1893-1945. Produced tablecloths, doilies, towels, handkerchiefs, silk textiles.

America's Pride, 1941-1963, Weil & Durrse (Wilendure). Produced tablecloths, linens, towels, napkins.

Aristocrat, 1950-1970. Produced tablecloth and napkin sets.

Bee Figural Logo, 1916-1967. Unknown manufacturer. Produced tablecloths, tray covers, bureau scarves made of linen.

Belccrest Linens, 1945-1965, Belcrest Linens, Corp., New York. Produced tablecloths and napkin sets. From 1950 to 1965 they were imported from Hong Kong.

Broderie Creations, 1940-1965. Produced tablecloths, napkins.

Brentmoore, 1921-1941, Ely Walker Dry Good, Missouri. Produced their own label for tablecloths and napkin sets.

Bucilla, 1919 to present.

Bur-Mil, 1940-1970, Burlington Mills Corp., North Carolina. Drapes, tablecloths, bedspreads.

Cactus Cloth, 1940-1970. Produced Souvenir tablecloth and napkin sets primarily on burlap material.

Calaprint, 1946-1968. Produced textile fabrics and table linens in California.

California Hand Prints, 1936-1969, California Hand Prints Inc. "Designed, Hand Screen Printed and Finished in Our Plant at Hermosa Beach, California." Maker of beach towels, tablecloths, clothing, and accessories.

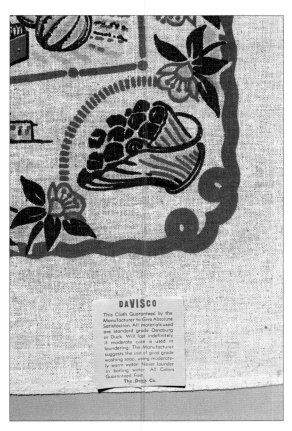

Callaway Mills, 1932-1950. In 1889, when he was eighteen, Fuller Callaway opened Fuller Callaway's Mammoth Department Store and eventually purchased the surrounding textile mills. Fuller's sons, Carson and Fuller Callaway, Jr., assumed leadership of the mills in 1920. In 1932, they restructured and consolidated the group of textile mills into the single corporation known as Callaway Mills, Inc. They produced tablecloths, doilies, linens, and towels until 1950.

Cannon, 1916 to present, Cannon Mills, North Carolina. Produced tablecloths, napkins, drapes, pot holders. Cannon Mills company was an enterprise begun in 1906 by industrialist James William Cannon. Under the guidance of James Cannon's son, Charles, Cannon Mills came to be known as the world's largest producer of household textiles, producing sheets, towels, bedspreads, etc. They merged in 1985 with Fieldcrest Mills Inc., making Fieldcrest Cannon a world leader in household textiles. Fieldcrest Cannon was purchased by the Pillowtex Corporation in 1997 but retained the Fieldcrest Cannon name.

Charm Prints, 1939-1959, Columbus-Union Oil Cloth Company. Began by producing oilcloth tablecloths in 1929. In late 1940s, they added a line of printed tablecloths.

Crown Figural Design with words "Ely Walker," Ely Walker Dry Goods, Missouri. Produced tablecloths, napkins, carpets, handkerchiefs.

Crown Figural Design with letters GJ, 1936-1967, George Jensen Inc., New York. Produced sheets, pillowcases, tablecloths, blankets.

Davisco. 1950s label states "Originators and Distributors of originals in Novelty, Domestic Cotton Print Linens. Specialists in Barbecue Linens — Souvenir Map Luncheon Cloths, Western Design Table Coverings. This Cloth Guaranteed by the Manufacturer to Give Absolute Satisfaction. All Materials used are standard grade Osnaburg or Duck."

Dunmoy, 1953-1970, Stevens and Sons Ltd., Ireland. Produced tablecloths, napkins, glass cloths, tea cloths, tray, and cocktail cloths.

E, 1949-1961, Emporium Capwell, San Francisco, California. Produced tablecloths, table tapestries, bunting, furniture scarves.

E & W, 1906-1969, Ely Walker Dry Goods, Missouri. Produced their own line of printed tablecloths. President George Walker Bush's great-grandfather.

Edsonart, 1944, Edson Incorp., Chicago, Illinois. Card Table covers, piece goods, cotton linen, and synthetic fibers.

Everfast, 1921-1972, Everfast Fabrics, Inc., New York. Produced tablecloths, drapes, napkins, tablemats.

Favorite Things, 1950 to present. Springs Industries, Fort Mill, South Carolina. Tablecloths, runners, dish and tea towels.

Fieldcrest, 1946 - , Fieldcrest Cannon, Inc. Purchased from Marshall Fields department store, Chicago. Tablecloths, linens, and gift sets. *[[Note 20]]*

First Lady, 1935 to present. Mercantile Stores Company, New York. Produces tablecloths, Turkish towels, printed dish cloths.

Garden State House of Prints, 1950-1980.

Gold Label, 1961-1981, Cannon Mills Corp., North Carolina. Tablecloths, coverlets, napkins.

Gold Medal Brand, 1893-1949, William Liddell, Co., Chicago, London, Dublin. Produced tablecloths, tray cloths, damasks, tea cloths, supper cloths, sideboard cloths, basin cloths.

Gribbons, Styled by Gribbons, 1923-1968, Gribbon Company, New York. Plain and embroidered linen and damask tablecloths.

Gumps, 1939-1968, S & G Gump Company, California. Produced tablecloths, napkins, placemats, drapes.

Hadon, 1945-1970, Haddad & Sons Inc., New York. Produced tablecloths, scarves, and clothing.

Happy Home, 1957-1976, F.W. Woolworths, New York. Produced tablecloths and curtains.

Hard-o-craft, 1950 to present. James Hardy & Co. Produced tablecloths, napkins, table runners, doilies, placemats.

Hardy Tex, 1939, James G. Hardy & Co. Produced tablecloths, napkins, table runners, doilies, placemats.

Hardycraft, 1923 to present. James G. Hardy & Co., Inc. Produced tablecloth and napkin sets, towels, and other kitchen textiles.

G. Hardy & Company, 1923 to present. Supplier of hotel and restaurant linens.

Harmony House. Sears' own label produced tablecloths and other household goods from 1940 to 1960.

Harwood Steiger Inc., 1956 to present. Harwood Steiger was a prominent western fabric designer from 1956 until his death in 1980. He created hand printed, silk-screened fabrics, suitable for clothing, draperies, wall hangings, etc. He also sold linen dish towels, tablecloths, and placemats. Steiger's sister-in-law still sells his wonderful designs in a small shop in Arizona.

Hawaiiprint, 1963 to present, Hawaii Print Corp., Hawaii. Bed linens, tablecloth sets made from woven and knit fabrics

Heirloom, 1950-1970, Bates Manufacturing Company, Maine. Known for their great 1950s bedspreads, they also produced tablecloths and napkins.

Indian Head Mills, founded in 1835 in Boston, Massachusetts. In 1898, the mill was moved to South Carolina. In the 1900 census, the town's population was shown as 567. Due to the success of the mill, the population rose in 1910 to 1,747. The cotton mill closed in 1963.

Lamb, Tom. Tom Lamb (1897-1985) was born in New York City. He studied at the Art Students League and New York University. In the 1920s, Lamb wrote and illustrated children's books and had a monthly page in *Good Housekeeping* magazine called "Kiddyland Movies," which spawned a line of children's products and kitchen textiles.

Lancaster Cotton Mills, 1895-1914. Lancaster Prints, Springs Industries 1914 to present. Leroy Springs established the mill in Lancaster, South Carolina.

Leacock Quality Prints, 1950-1969, New York. Produced tablecloths, napkins.

Leda, 1951-1971, Leda Lee Design, California. Produced tablecloths and other kitchen textiles.

Martex, 1930 to present, WestPoint Stevens Inc., South Carolina. One of the oldest textile mills in the South, this company is currently made up of three textile giants from the past. J.P Stevens is the company's oldest name, dating back to 1813. Pepperell Manufacturing Company Inc. was founded in 1851 in Biddeford, Maine. Incorporated in 1880, West Point Manufacturing Company was based in West Point, Georgia. In 1965, West Point and Pepperell merged. Stevens was acquired in 1988.

Maytex, 1944-1990, Maytex Mills, Inc., New York. Produced house wares, tablecloths, placemats, kitchen towels.

ML Cloth, 1950-1970. Produced tablecloths and napkins.

Mosse, 1916-1965, Mosse Inc. Produced tablecloths, linens, blankets for the yachting industry.

Nileen, 1947-1968, Simtex Mills, New York. Produced tablecloths, napkins.

Parisian Prints, 1960 - present. Produced tablecloths, souvenir tablecloths.

Pennicraft, 1946-1975. J.C. Penney's own label of tablecloths and other kitchen textiles.

Pine Tree Linens, 1927-1947. Produced tablecloths, luncheon sets, doilies, card table sets, breakfast sets, dinner sets.

Pride Of Flanders, 1930-1970 Specialized in "Irish Linens."

Prints Charming, 1963-1985, Sun Weave Linen Corp., New York. Produced tablecloths, napkins, linens.

Printex, 1936 to present. Company founded in 1936 by Vera and her husband to produce "Vera" line and other "art" linens.

Prismacolor G&W, 1970-1985 (spinning wheel logo). Produced tablecloths and towels.

Rosemary, 1922 to present, Rosemary Manufacturing, New York. Produced table linens, damasks, jacquard woven fabrics. Purchased by J.P Stephens in the 1980s.

Royal Household, 1906-1969, Cannon Mills Co., Inc. Produced tablecloths, napkins, and bedspreads.

Setting Pretty, 1944-1962. Weil & Durrse, Inc. (Wilendure), New York, produced this line of tablecloths, napkins, placemats, towels, cotton pieces.

Simtex, 1946-1968, a division of Simmons Co., 40 Worth Street, New York. Produced tablecloths, bedspreads, upholstery, and plain piece goods. Purchased by J.P. Stevens in the 1960s.

Springmaid, 1887 to present. Springs Industries was founded in 1887 as Fort Mill Manufacturing Company in Fort Mill, South Carolina, by Samuel Elliott

White. In 1919, Spring Maid cotton mills operated five textile mills in South Carolina as separate companies: Fort Mill Plant, White Plant, Lancaster Plant, Kershaw Plant, and Eureka Plant. In 1933, all the plants were incorporated into The Springs Cotton Mills. In 1947, they began producing tablecloths and napkins along with their household textile products. Now known as Spring Industries.

Stalwart, 1947-1970, R.H. Macy Co., New York. Produced tablecloths, sheets, pillowcases. Used Indian Head Cotton.

Startex (with "star" incorporated into design), 1920-1945; Startex (without "star"), 1945-2001, Startex Mills, South Carolina. Printed tablecloths, kitchen towels. Purchased by Reigel Textile Corp in the 1960s. Now owned by the Clifton Manufacturing Company.

State Pride, 1954 to present, Belk Stores Services Inc., North Carolina. Produces tablecloths, aprons, bedspreads, drapes, coverlets, towels.

STC (Standard Textile Company), 1942-1979, Standard Textile Co., Ohio. Produced tablecloths, sheets, toweling, huck towels.

Tanvald, 1921-1967, Hermann & Jacobs Corp., New York. Produced tablecloths and napkins from fine linen and cotton.

The Emporium, 1896-1949, San Francisco, California. Emporium Capwell produced tablecloths, table tapestries, bunting, furniture scarves.

The Linen Of Queens, 1948-1975, D. Porthoult Inc., New York. Household linens, tablecloths, napkins.

Thomas Gold Label Print, 1950 to present. Produced tablecloth and napkins.

Thomaston, 1927 to present, Thomaston Cotton Mills, Georgia. Produced cotton and damask tablecloths and napkins.

Thomaston Mills, 1899 to present, Thomaston, Georgia. In 1899, a group of local investors led by Robert E. Hightower, whose family had been in Georgia since before the American Revolution, chartered Thomaston Cotton Mills. There was cotton in abundance and access to railroads. By the 1950s, the company employed the best textile stylist in the industry (according to a corporate history) and went after the discount market just as colored home textiles were coming into vogue.

Vera, 1935 to present, Vera Inc., Los Angeles, California. Produced tablecloths, napkins, scarves, and clothing.

Vicray, 1946-1966, Kemp & Beatley, New York. Produced tablecloth sets.

Victory, 1919-1940, Kemp & Beatley, New York. Produced tablecloths, doilies, and table covers.

Victory (figural crown), K & B, 1919-1972, Kemp & Beatley, New York. Tablecloth protectors, pads.

Wifitex. 1950s tablecloth manufacturer.

Wilendur, 1939-1958, Weil & Durrse, New York. Produced tablecloths, napkins, placemats, runners.

Wilendure, 1958-1990, Weil & Durrse, New York. Produced tablecloths, napkins, placemats, runners.

Yucca Prints, 1930 to present, Barth & Dreyfuss, Los Angeles, California. Produced souvenir and "Western" style tablecloths and napkin sets from 1930 to 1960. Still produces products for home furnishings. Barth & Dreyfuss of California designs, manufactures, and distributes high quality kitchen and bath decor.

Chapter 11

Useful Resources

On-line Stores

There are a vast number of vintage tablecloth and linen dealers on the web. Just typing in "vintage linens" or "vintage tablecloths" in your search engine will give you hours and hours of shopping pleasure from the comfort of your own computer. Here are a few of my favorite on-line dealers, and of course, you can buy vintage linens and tablecloths on almost all of the popular "on-line auction sites" as well.

Easy Street Antiques
www.easystreetantiques.com

Vintage textiles, including tablecloths, runners, towels, hankies, lace, fabric, and scarves.

Grama's Attic Linens
www.gramasattic.com

Specializes in vintage tablecloths, vintage kitchen textiles, and specialty boutique items made from vintage linens.

Mama Whiskas House o' Goodies
www.mamawiskas.com

Caters to the discriminating vintage connoisseur, specializing in the finest textiles. Also offers a wide variety of other retro accessories and kitchenware to add just the right finishing touches to any cottage chic decor.

Retro Redheads
www.retro-redheads.com

An on-line catalogue of vintage housewares "for the Modern Gal & Dapper Guy"—includes Fire King, Jadite, Pyrex, vintage kitchen textiles, Red & White Kitchen line of retro style linens, twentieth century dinnerware, barware, and much more.

Reprodepot Fabrics
www.reprodepotfabrics.com
206-938-5585

Specializes in vintage reproduction fabrics, tablecloths, trimmings, housewares, and gifts.

Sharon's Antiques Vintage Fabrics
http://www.rickrack.com
610-756-6048

Inventory includes vintage and antique cotton fabrics, feedsacks, quilts, and quilt blocks; also kitchen towels, aprons, hankies, and vintage printed tablecloths.

The Vintage Table
www.thevintagetable.net

Specializes in printed linens from the 1930s through the 1960s. These gorgeous linens have given decades of pleasure to families and now bring a touch of whimsy to your everyday table.

Collectors' Club

The *Vintage Tablecloth Lover's Club* is dedicated to the preservation and interpretation of the history and heritage of vintage kitchen textiles. The Club was established in the late summer of 2002 by enthusiasts of 1930s-1950s vintage printed tablecloths. The club's purpose is to promote the education and appreciation of these pieces of "Kitchen Textile Art" from our past, as well as to have fun sharing our hobby and creating lasting friendships in a secure, on-line club room. More information can be found at www.vintagetableclothsclub.com

Glossary

Aniline Dyes. Chemical dyes (as opposed to vegetable ones) derived from coal tar. These were developed for use in the late 1850s.

Cactus Cloth. Trademarked name used by Barth and Dreyfuss to describe a soft burlap type material.

Damask. A fabric of silk, rayon, and cotton or other combinations of fibers woven in jacquard weave with reversible flat designs.

Dry Goods. An early marketing term for textile fabrics.

Dyestuff. Dyes used for printing color on textiles.

Fugitive. An unstable dye that tends to run, fade, or change colors.

Ghost Fabric. A textile that contained a fugitive dye, leaving no color or only a little color. This condition is most often seen in some red and green dyes as well as pinks and blues from the 1850s to the 1930s.

Homespun. A very coarse, rough linen, wool, cotton or man-made fiber or blend in varied colors, generally in a plain weave.

Linen. This is the strongest of the vegetable fibers and has two to three times the strength of cotton. It is made from flax, a bast fiber taken from the stalk of the plant. The luster is from the natural wax content. Creamy white to light tan, this fiber can be easily dyed and the color does not fade when washed. Linen does wrinkle easily.

Madder. A shrubby herb grown for the dyeing properties of its root. Madder is the basic colorant for Turkey Red and the coppery browns of the late 1800s.

Mercerization. Originally developed by John Mercer about 1850, mercerization was forgotten until 1890 when the idea was patented. It is a process that gives an increase in flexibility, strength, and luster to cotton tablecloths. It was advertised on tablecloths produced between 1920 and 1940.

Mordant. A chemical agent that fixes a dyestuff to a fiber.

Over Dyed/Over Printed. A tablecloth that was vat dyed in two different baths, or stamped first with one color then stamped or over printed with another to create a third color.

Rayon. Made from cellulose, rayon has many of the qualities of cotton, a natural cellulose fiber. Rayon is strong, extremely absorbent, comes in a variety of qualities and weights, and can be made to resemble natural fabrics. Rayon does not melt but burns at high temperatures. Kenneth Lord, Sr. coined the word "rayon" in 1924 during an industry sponsored contest to find a name for what was then known as "artificial silk."

Sailcloth. A generic name for fabrics used for sails. It is usually made of cotton, linen, jute, or nylon and is a heavy, almost canvas-feeling fabric. Favorite fabric of both Wilendur and Startex.

Sanforized. Trade name of a process for shrinkage control, meaning residual shrinkage of not over 1% guaranteed. It was developed in the 1950s and advertised on some tablecloth tags during that time.

Tapestry. A jacquard woven fabric in cotton, wool, or man-made fibers. The design is woven in by means of colored filling yarns. On the back, shaded stripes identify this fabric.

Turkey Red. A specific shade of red produced from the madder plant. The technique involved placing fabric in an oil bath. A colorfast dye, it was first developed in Turkey. Turkey red can fade to pink with use.

Bibliography

Bosker, Gideon and Michele Mancici. *Fabulous Fabrics of the 50's*. San Francisco, California: Chronicle Books, 1992.

Carmichael, W.L., Linton, George E., and Isaac Price. *Callaway Textile Dictionary*. La Grange, Georgia: Callaway Mills, 1947.

Glasell, Pamela. *Collectors' Guide to Vintage Tablecloths*. Atglen, Pennsylvania: Schiffer Publishing, Ltd., 2002.

Jessup, Elon. *The Motor Camping Book*. New York, New York: G.P. Putnam's Sons, 1921.

Johnson, George H. *Textile Fabrics*. New York, New York: Harper & Brothers, 1927.

Johnston, Meda Parker, and G. Kaufman. *Design on Fabrics*. New York, New York: Van Nostrand Reinhold Company, 1967.

Meller, Susan and Joost Elffers. *Textile Designs*. New York, New York: Harry N. Abrams, Inc., 1991.

Shaffer, Marguerite S. *See America First: Tourism And National Identity 1880-1940*. Washington, D.C.: Smithsonian Institution Press, 2001.

Smith, Loretta Fehling. *Terrific Tablecloths from the '40s & '50s*. Atglen, Pennsylvania: Schiffer Publishing Ltd., 1998.

Wilson, Kax. *A History of Textiles*. Boulder, Colorado: Westview Press, Inc., 1979.

Wingate, Isabel. *Textile Fabrics and Their Selection*. New York, New York: Prentice-Hall, 1949.